SPOKEN FOR

Unearthing God's Relentless Love and Ending the
Cycle of Heartbreak

STEPHANIE HAZLE LYLE

DAYELight
PUBLISHERS

ISBN: 978-1-966723-04-2 (paperback)

Dedication

I would like to dedicate this book to my family, especially to my mother. I am very grateful for the selfless woman she was, for her strengths, weaknesses, and unwavering faith in Christ, and for every good thing she unremittingly passed on to me. She is my inspiration, especially considering the ways she experienced heartbreak throughout her life. In spite of that, she represented a woman of faith in God and unconditional love for people.

Acknowledgments

I am thankful to my heavenly Father for giving me a place in His family through Christ Jesus, who continues to show me true love daily.

I pray anyone reading this book will have a genuine relationship with Christ. May you walk in step with Him as you pursue relationships and be guided by Him always.

I also want to thank one of my best friends and mentor, Dexter, who has been telling me to write my story for a long time.

To my late mother, Elaine Hazle (June 26, 1960 - September 11, 2024)

Preface

I am not yet a parent, but I observed my mother and father while helping with my siblings for years. As the eldest child of four, I realised that parenting is one of life's greatest challenges and most assuredly requires intervention from a Higher, Greater Force.

This book is not about parenting but will largely explore the striking correlation between our parent-child experiences and how we navigate relationships, specifically romantic ones.

I believe one of the greatest blessings in my life has been the gift of faith, which has allowed me to be aware of a tangible relationship with God from my preteen years. While this was the case, I was not spared the consequences of occasionally choosing to live independently of this relationship. Having experienced failed relationships where the value systems were undeniably incompatible from the very start, or where I was seeking to fulfil my own desires at both of our expense, whether or not there was already a girlfriend in the picture, or where my suitor's ugly, abusive streak showed itself in the worst way, I finally asked God: "Why do I keep doing this?" "This" being the habit of choosing questionable relationships that ultimately end in heartbreak.

That moment began the journey to recognize my need for divine intervention. It was a need to really feel God's love and receive His healing. By His grace, I have grown more self-aware and attuned to the multiple factors in my life that influenced my decision-making in past relationships. The truth was simple: I had been searching for genuine and constant love in a partner, and although I knew God and believed that He loved me, did I really grasp the fullness of His love for me in every part of my being? Did I believe that God, who so loved me, also wanted to see me become united with a man after His heart who would be the right match for me?

We all have different stories that contribute to the fascinating people we are, but what if our childhood was shaped through the full assurance of being adored children of the Most High God? How different would our stories be? What if we learned biblical truths about our identity earlier in life? How would that have affected decisions we made later in life? It is stirring to ponder, but better than pondering what we cannot change, we can now affirm, learn, and perhaps unlearn as much as possible while helping to equip the generations to come.

I hope this book will impact you as you truly receive God's love and share it with persons, especially those who feel unloved. There is One who loves us deeply, and only He provides a sure path to inner healing of every kind of emotional pain. You can rest assured He wants you to have only the best as you navigate the world of romance and prepare for marriage, so hold on to His hand as you go out there and trust Him with your love life.

Every day, remind yourself of this affirmation:

"I am loved by my heavenly Father with an everlasting love. There is no one who can take this right away from me, not even myself. Anyone who wants to gain entry into my life has to receive the approval of my Father, for I am Spoken For."

Have you ever experienced a break-up and felt like you were at the end of yourself? You gave so much of yourself over time, and now you are grappling with unmet expectations. Are you buried under the weight of disappointment in people and yourself? Maybe you have been in a relationship with the same person who managed to crush you emotionally over and over again.

If you can identify with any of these scenarios, you are probably suffering from what this book calls "heartbreak." There are many ways to define that condition, but I will put it this way:

> *Broken-heartedness is that state of being when we are so deeply wounded internally that it significantly affects our wellness emotionally, mentally, spiritually, and physically, even to the point of complete desensitisation where we don't readily recognise the broken state of our heart.*

For many people, including Christians, heartbreak can be lost on us as we tell ourselves that, "We are fine." Furthermore, we are aware that "God loves us and blah blah blah." I know; I have been there when I didn't want to turn to the Bible for comfort but needed God to reach down from heaven Himself and hold me in His arms. Beloved, I understand that kind of pain, and while I can't promise that reading this book will magically remove the hurt, my prayer is that it would help the eyes of your heart to be even more open to embracing the unrelenting love that your heavenly Father has for you.

Table of Contents

Introduction...13

Chapter 1: Return to Sender 17

   Carnal Versus Spirit..32

   Prayer of Repentance of Unrighteous Relationships 36

   Prayer When There is Anger Towards God..........................37

Chapter 2: I Am Spoken For......................................39

   A Secret Wish...53

   Air Hug 54

   Strong Man 56

   Prayer During Emotional Pain...................................59

Chapter 3: An Audit of the Heart 61

   Love, Your Father 80

Chapter 4: The Rocky Road to Restored 83

   A Happy Girl's Sadness 95

   Hate Is The Worst Disease 97

   Again 99

   Whole-Hearted Love 101

Chapter 5: Singleness, My SuperPower 105

   Sweet Feeling 111

   Prince of Peace, Prince of Power............................113

Chapter 6: Born to Belong (God Made Us For Community) . 115

   Nothing Matters 124

Chapter 7: Obedience Over Sacrifice 129

Chapter 8: Faithfulness Yields Fruit 137

   Spoken For By God 154

Epilogue 159

   Indescribable Feeling 164

About the Author 169

Introduction

I wrote this book because there are many life lessons I have been learning for over a decade on practical ways to navigate heartbreak from broken relationships that I feel compelled to share. Not that there is a formula, but I do believe there are some steps to prevent or cope with excruciatingly painful situations as a result of the loss of a romantic relationship. Invariably, the content may also extend to those hurting from the loss of a loved one, dealing with unmet expectations in relationships, unrequited love, and mourning the loss of something you once treasured, like a job, valuable item, or even your health. Whatever we have faced that would cause us to be down-hearted, Christ, the Lord and Saviour of the world, faced a variation of the same while He lived on earth. He faced betrayal, false accusation of the highest degree, being denied by His closest friends, and physical, mental, and emotional agony for the sake of saving the lives of those He loved, that is, all of mankind.

> *"But God demonstrates his own love for us in this: While we were still sinners, Christ died for us." (Romans 5:8 – NIV).*

Jesus' resurrection from death is the physical manifestation and most vivid reminder that, with God in charge of our lives, there is victory on the other end of suffering—it does not last forever and is never in vain. The painful circumstances we survive are not wasted, and if we give our pain to Him, He will not only heal us, but He will ensure that whatever was meant to harm us will be used to serve purpose in our lives and the lives of others.

As human beings, our experiences often affect not just us but at least one other person in some way. We are connected to each other by God's design. It is important then for us to pay more attention to the roots of our pain and give more of our attention to the only one who can heal and make us whole. Yes, there is one who is able to do so despite the examples of care-giving you may have been shown or taught.

Maybe you are against the reality of the existence of a Saviour because instead of being shown love, you were physically or emotionally abandoned or even abused. You have become self-reliant, operating as your own saviour, or found your hope in the creation instead of the Creator. If this is you, then this is an invitation to a new perspective because, in truth, you have never left the sight of the heavenly Father. Though your pain may be justified due to the failings of people, even those who were appointed to care for you, God is powerful and mighty to intercept the core belief cycle. He will transform you into a brand new person, inside-out, to activate your full purpose as the child who belongs to Him, able to love others in the way Christ does, including those who have hurt you. It takes the indwelling of the Spirit of God, which happens when we give our lives to Jesus.

I declare that through this divinely inspired book, millions of people will come into close intimacy with and dependency on Christ and experience great healing and breakthrough in their pursuit of godly marriage, in Jesus' name.

Chapter 1

Return to Sender

"And everyone who thus hopes in Him purifies himself as He is pure." (1 John 3:3 – NIV).

The word *purity* meant nothing to me until my mid-twenties. Before that time, it was not a part of my vocabulary and held no place in my thoughts. I vaguely remember schoolmates referring to purity rings at my "uptown" all–girls catholic high school with parents who sought to brand their daughters as virginal, maybe for their own peace of mind more than anything else. While I admired the concept then, no part of me had ever considered it relevant personally. Only since I have gotten older and matured in my journey as a Christian have I come to appreciate the importance of observing chastity as a young woman and how essential it is to learn its value as early as possible, difficult as it is in a world where sex is heavily commercialised and meaningless to many.

What made the difference for me was recognising my desperate state and understanding who I was in the eyes of my heavenly Father, my Creator. That was when I started to view myself differently in light of being pure. I began to appreciate that in the presence of a holy God, nothing that is defiled or corrupted is acceptable. But does that not rule us all out of ever being able to stand in the presence of God? The answer is, *"Yes, it would,"* but the better answer is, *"That is why Jesus paid the price He did on the cross, and now anyone who is willing to believe in Him and confess this truth can stand boldly before the Father, flaws and all, knowing that Jesus has qualified us."*

You may find it strange that a book on how to heal from a broken heart would start with the subject of purity, but I promise, stick with me, and it might just be as transformational for you as it has been for me.

We live in a world where people have been deeply wounded and disenfranchised, having lost agency over themselves in one way or another, whether due to their environment, upbringing and family life, peer interactions, exposure to any forms of manipulation and abuse, and the list goes on. The result is a people, particularly in the western cultural context, obsessed with their rights, that is, an idea of freedom where people can do as they will in defiance of the forces that have sought to control them. What the Bible teaches about freedom is that, firstly, God is just and therefore advocates for justice. The interesting thing about freedom, through the lens of the Bible, is its connection to the act of presenting our bodies as a living sacrifice to God (see Romans 12:1), which basically means surrendering our desires and yielding to what God wants. Our opposition and rebellion against this view are indicators of every human being's greatest form of brokenness, that is, bondage to our sinful, rebellious nature. Only a living and breathing relationship with Christ can break such bondage, and purity becomes more central to being able to pick up the pieces when life's blows strike.

Here is how it may start to make sense even to the most liberal-minded person: our bodies, that is, the physical and immaterial elements (spirit and soul) of our makeup, become deeply affected when we go through any form of heartache (be it after ten days or ten years), betrayal, the breaking of trust, loss of a loved one or something you treasured, like a job. The gravity of each experience may vary and can depend on different factors that may not be obvious to you. For example, you could be undergoing chronic or complex trauma without realising you have just been through so many different negative experiences over a prolonged period to the point where you have become numb. Each experience has chipped away at your very being. Eventually, you become but a shell of yourself—emotionally speaking—so anything even slightly distressing could *"Lick yuh for six,"* as we say in Jamaica, referencing our love of the sport of cricket. Basically, what would ordinarily seem like a small thing could hit very hard. The crazy part is that someone could still be highly functional as far as the eye can see, but they are in complete shambles on the inside. Sounds familiar, right? Yes, we all can identify with this in some way—some people can relate more than others. The fact is, whether you are a pro-mask-wearer or not, we can only maintain the facade for so long, and eventually, what is rotting on the inside begins to surface, and well, we know what happens when something starts to rot—the stench can be unbearable.

Perhaps what really propelled me onto the path of this kind of introspection was when I was twenty-one years old. I had my first significant broken heart from a romantic relationship. Others later followed, but at this particular juncture, I was at a point where my sense of identity was completely blurred. I had spent the first three years of my young adult life in a relationship—we literally made it official on my 18th birthday—and our lives were so intertwined that we could hardly imagine ourselves apart. He was a marketing major, and I was studying media and communication. So we managed to be separate during our classes, even though on occasion, I would neatly fit myself in his lectures whenever I had free time. When we got our results after the first semester exams, he had passed all his courses with flying colours while I failed two of mine. We did everything together and accompanied each other everywhere. Looking back, we were either a really cute couple or a really clingy pair.

I committed my life fully to Christ and got baptised at nineteen years old, which meant significant changes in the relationship. When we had to deal with infidelity as a couple, we could not muster the courage to separate, even if that was the healthy choice in the matter. We were in college, and he lived conveniently close to our school, so I spent most of those three years in his home; I was pretty much part of the family. He was fortunate to have been given a car by his parents at the relatively young age of eighteen, which meant early independence for him while I depended on him to take me everywhere: singing engagements, link-ups with friends and family members, parties—everywhere. We were the definition of "batty and bench," that is, inseparable. Even so, our relationship was not immune to the many ways young relationships are affected by issues like insecurity and mistrust, which slowly eroded the foundation of our bond over time. I remember a time when he seemed irrationally wound up about a coworker from my summer job who liked me. Maybe I naively shared about this person, and I verbalised that I had enforced clear boundaries, but still, I was somehow made to feel like I was to blame for the man's attraction. I had been too pleasant, or I was too nice, so it was my fault. I came to realise that a sign of someone who is guilty is that they are overly accusatory.

When school resumed after that summer, one day, I was in my class packing up as the day had ended. I was about to shut down my computer when I saw a message appear on Facebook. The person's message read something like, *"Your boyfriend slept with my girlfriend, and she just told me everything."* Having never been in a situation like that before, I froze in front of my screen, rereading the message several times over just in case. I might have typed a message back in response, but I was in such shock at the time that I cannot recall any words. The good thing is my close friend was pretty much next to me, waiting for me to gather my things so we

21

could both depart when she noticed my paused state. She came over to the screen and, shortly after, kept repeating, *"No, no... this cannot be happening to you guys... I do not believe he would do this."* I did not believe it either, to be honest, to the point where I convinced myself that it was not true and it was just a product of another couple's toxic relationship. I was so confident of this that when it was time to go home, we got in the car, and I told my boyfriend about the Facebook message somewhat casually, only for him to turn a shade whiter than his usual caucasian-black mixed shade as he sat in the driver's seat beside me, unable to hold eye contact as his hands gripped the steering wheel. All he could manage to say with tear-filled eyes was, *"We will talk about this when we get to the house."* What was a five-minute drive felt like an endless ride. The silence was deafening, and yet it said it all as if his obvious reaction to my casual mention did not say enough.

In the hours that followed, I experienced a mixture of emotions that were strange to me: inadequacy, insecurity, rage, sadness, and empathy all in one. I had never been "cheated on" before; after all, this relationship was my first serious one. Sure, theoretically, I had an idea of how painful this kind of betrayal might be, but at the same time, I did not feel as angry as I expected. That may have been because of how he spent the uncomfortable hours making calls on speakerphone to individuals, including his female friend he had cheated with and her estranged boyfriend who had messaged me, pretty much apologising, reiterating to them how much he loved me. I had never seen it displayed like that in the movies, so this was truly novel. Whether or not it was his motive, at that moment, I was not given the space to be angry. Between trying to absorb the reality of this disappointment and being smothered by apologies, I really could not fully process what was happening. I was being flooded by intense emotions, both his and my own, and I could hardly stay afloat. It was an experience that I will never forget.

Needless to say, we did not break up upon this occurrence. After a few days to myself, with a bit more time to think more clearly, call me foolish, but I chose forgiveness, knowing that I too had made mistakes. The most painful part of everything was really the fact that I found out the way I did, and I was taken so off guard. It would be work to rebuild trust and to see past his dishonesty, knowing that if I hadn't gotten that Facebook message, I may never have known the truth, but I made my decision, and we continued in the relationship for about another year and a half.

When that relationship ended, it felt like I had entered a different world—the kind of world where I no longer bore the identity of his girlfriend. I had become so used to being widely identified in this way among our peers that it was hard for me to imagine myself as anyone else. Now I was just Stephanie: single and ready to mingle? I felt more like fresh meat flung to a pack of wolves, no longer hidden in the shelter of the relationship. Of course, a part of me also felt liberated as I knew I was about to (re)discover who I was and meet new people without having to explain myself to anyone. However, without the presence of strong male guidance at that time, my life spiralled into a season of meaningless 'situation-ships' as I sought after that safe place I so needed, giving away precious parts of myself out of vulnerability and deep longing for male intimacy. This was an opening to an intense attraction to someone more than twice my age in the aftermath of my breakup. It started as a genuine friendship, complete with ongoing conversations about shared interests like songs we both loved, poems we had both enjoyed and written, occasional drive-outs, and exploring new restaurants for lunch. He was someone who was poised to be a mentor with all the insight and value he added to my life effortlessly and generously; to add to that, he had known what it was like to go through a breakup after a long-term relationship, and his support during that period was truly invaluable. But what may have been initially innocent turned into a romantic connection unexpectedly—although looking back, if we had both been more discerning, it would not have come as a surprise to either of us—with a man who was technically unavailable in many ways and one who did not share my beliefs. More than that was the fact that I was utterly broken and distraught, though distracted by the newness of this friendship, but the reality of the breakup caught up to me, and I made the painfully necessary decision to put an end to whatever was ensuing between us.

What was also hard to resist was the urge to fight against feeling the pain of the loss of the person who I was closest to for the last three years, who essentially was now treating me like a stranger because, for him, breakups were final and required limited to no contact. I died a thousand deaths when I went out and saw him with other women, having the time of his life without me. Even if I happened to have been there with someone else too, banking on the chance of making him jealous or missing me, that would not stop me from being an emotional trainwreck. Thanks to the music blaring across the venue, the noisy bathrooms at these events were my respite. Empty cubicles that reeked of urine became my place of refuge, where I could holler as hard and bawl as loud as I wanted without being seen or heard.

Even while going through what was my lowest moment when my self-worth felt extinct, a part of me still knew somehow that I was special, and that my life was not made to look or feel the way it did. That bit of hope allowed me to take my broken self and stagger to Bible Study with my friend, who sweetly begged me to accompany her. She was not aware of how much more desperate than her I was when I eagerly accepted her invitation—a friend in need is truly a friend indeed. When your life feels like a mess, and your self-esteem is below ground zero, consider it an opportunity to (re)learn the fundamentals of who you are. It is a chance to go back to the drawing board.

Those Bible Studies allowed me to sit in the comfort of women of varying ages and stages of life—some had children, some were heads of their own companies, others were leaders in organisations, some a little older than me and just embarking on their careers, some battled lifelong illnesses, some were divorced, others single and married. Eventually, there was nothing I looked forward to in my week more than meeting at these women's seemingly perfectly organised homes, experiencing the loving hospitality, warmth, and good spiritual food while digesting delightful actual food during our study times. We took turns bringing snacks ranging from chips and homemade hummus by one of the women with Middle Eastern roots to freshly baked cakes and other sweet treats. We engaged in conversations about real-life scenarios and prayed to our God for His intervention in our situations. Walking hand in hand together with these women provided healing for me in so many ways. Eventually, I saw my life goals being reshaped and my understanding of my identity forming. I began to have a deeper appreciation for godly values according to the Bible, and that was the turning point in my life.

Purity is the quality of being blemish-free—uncorrupted. Purity occurs by a process of refining, where impurities are removed or filtered, making the element clean and beneficial. This has become one of those new important values I have learned over the years of prioritising being in the presence of God more, that is, making room to worship, meditating on the Word of God, and hearing from Him. As far as the clothes I wear, the music I listen to, the thoughts I entertained, the conversations I participate in, the list goes on—the song from my childhood comes to mind *"Watch your eyes, watch your eyes what they see. For there's a Father up above looking down with tender love, watch your eyes, watch your eyes what they see."*

Thankfully, observing purity is something that I now internalise as an integral part of who I am, not that I have mastered it. I certainly believe my life shows that it is possible to come from living a life guided by your own principles of right and wrong to being guided primarily by Biblical principles. I have to say, the latter has been a far more fulfilling and sensible way to go, though definitely more challenging. For example, I can remember entertaining ideas as a teen around "safe sex" without any real deep look at the foundation of sex and the context within which God created humans to engage in it. I believe I would have been better off learning about how neglecting sexual purity would bruise my relationship with God and separate me from Him further; how pre-marital sex, with or without contraceptives, would greatly complicate my life and affect my self-worth as it has the power to intensify the emotional struggles. I wish I had known how premarital sex would lead me on a path of destroying my mind and body and how I would develop dependencies that would only serve to bring me closer to death.

As we direct our focus towards solutions, imagine yourself as a high-end luxury vehicle that has been in an accident. What would be required to ensure it gets the best possible care so it can be made as good as new again? Ideally, it should be returned to its manufacturer and/or the representative of the manufacturer, or at the very least, a mechanic with a trained eye who can help restore the state of the vehicle. If you are following the analogy correctly, and I am crossing my fingers that you are, then you would have noticed that the manufacturer is our heavenly Father, the representative is Christ, and the one with a trained eye could be a pastor trained in counselling skills.

All of this may be linked to purity if you think of the word from which it derives, "pure," which means "complete and total." As you read, you will also see the reference to purity in light of one's cleansing of any thing that is not of God. The bottom line remains that in order to be completely restored (like a luxury vehicle), cleansed of impurities, and healed from life's hard blows (or dents, in this case), it means we have to go back to the basics, to the foundation of who we are at the core from God's perspective, as He is and will always be our Maker (Manufacturer).

As it turned out, purity was a very relevant thing to consider, and eventually, it consumed my thoughts. I became more convicted of every "little thing" and often asked myself, *"Does this thought honour God? Should I be in this setting? If I conduct myself in this particular way, will this bring glory to God? How does what I'm saying reflect Him as His daughter? Am I representing Christ?"*

The fact is, sexual immorality has been the cause of much of the degradation of our society on all fronts, and it starts with poisoning each of us, one by one. By sexual immorality, I am referring to every and any deviation from or denial of what is clearly stated in the Word of God around sex and sexuality. I understand this may be a sensitive subject for many, as it is for me, but this is one of the results of the devastation of living in a fallen world that is now tainted—against the desire of our Creator. Nevertheless, His Son, Jesus Christ, is the hope of the world, and what He did on the cross presents humanity with an escape from our grave predicament of being born under a sentence of death.

Another interesting thing I have noticed about sexual purity is that, outside of the governance of the Bible, it becomes incredibly subjective to the point where any and everything is permissible. We see this in the multitude of expressions of sexual orientations today and the dynamic gender ideologies that continue to evolve. As women, we convince ourselves that even though this is the fifth guy with whom we have been sexually intimate within two months, our behaviour is not promiscuous, pointing to the deeper cry of our hearts. For some women, there is the view that we live in a new era, and it is "liberating" for women to have sex as casually as they please.

The idea of female liberation being tied to a no-holds-barred approach to sex is not new or unique to the current era. Women and men alike have always (mis)used sex for purposes that served selfish desires and interests, whether it is "woman empowerment" or "male domination." Sex has been wielded to wreak all kinds of egocentric ambitions across the history of mankind. In the beginning of the Bible, which chronicles events that date as far back as 2000 BC (4000+ years ago), it is written that the daughters of Abraham's nephew, Lot, thought it was appropriate to get their father drunk and have sex with him in order to save their genealogy. According to the "14 Eras: Story of Sexual Brokenness" by Chronological Bible Teaching Ministries, God demonstrates His superior power over our carnality by not shielding us from knowing the truth of the history of sexual immorality. The sexually broken world of our ancestors is the same broken world we live in presently. None of what we see today is new. The good news is that God was powerful enough to break demonic strongholds then, and He alone can restore us now.

Human beings do not manufacture purity nor can it be determined on a subjective basis. It is not a matter of our opinion or our personal moral compasses but is defined by God, who has given His Word, penned by humans who He inspired. It is meant to be a guide for living in this world and a shield of protection from anything we may face. Being able to live pure lives depends solely upon how much we believe and obey the Word of God and whether or not our heart posture is right towards God.

Are you angry with God? Do you struggle with believing that He is equally sovereign as He is good? Have we accepted that His will for our lives is by far the only way that will lead to true fulfilment on earth and life in eternity with Him? Through reflection and deeper connection with our Maker, the sovereign God who is holy, we develop a desire to be blameless in His eyes. Prior to this kind of conviction, purity will likely be viewed as unattainable and unnecessary. It might even be frowned upon as it can be wrongfully associated with being prudish and legalistic.

Purity is embodied in the person of Christ, who was and is the only sinless person. While we are not expected to be perfect, through His Spirit, we do have the opportunity to be supernaturally transformed into leading lifestyles that are beautiful and pure, but it must start at the heart level first and then manifest outwardly.

CARNAL VERSUS SPIRIT

Carnal:
Tell me, how do I stay pure
With a mind that's unclean
A body with hormones that scream
With a heart that belongs to You
Yet willing to give in
Towards a natural inclination
To this thing called sin.
I want to be pleased, and please,
Express how I feel with ease
Without this weight of knowing
That the direction I'm going
Takes me further away from You.
I see the caution signs
Amber lights glare at me
But I proceed without steering
Away from the danger that waits.
In this moment, my cravings I feed
Not caring enough about
where my actions will lead.

Spirit:
Before I hit the crater ahead,
And fall deep into an everlasting hole,
A voice resonates inside my soul.

I realise my strong will takes me too far,
Further than I am prepared to go
And before I get there,
where I will feel abandoned and alone
Grace reminds me who I am
and more importantly
Who He is.
I will reap the fruits of my purity
I will stay true to the one I serve
Through faith and works.
My own strength fails me
So with a mind that's renewed
And a body that's Your temple,
With a heart that still belongs to You
That won't be willing to give in
Towards a natural inclination
To this thing called sin,
I win.

PERSONAL REFLECTION

1. What would you say are your top five values that are most important to you in relationships?

2. How did you handle a time when you felt overwhelmed by the temptation to go against your values?

3. Have you ever felt pressured by people or by your circumstances to commit an act that went against your beliefs? Describe it here.

4. What are some values you believe are important to God in your relationship with Him and with others?

5. What are the differences between your values and God's?

6. Have you ever had an experience where you knew a relationship was not right, but you continued in it, which ultimately led to regret? Share about it here. Take a moment to confess it to God and receive His grace and forgiveness. (Say the Prayer of Repentance of Unrighteous Relationships on page 36).

7. Have you ever felt frustrated with trying to meet God's standards? Explain here.

Looking at these verses of the Bible, write down what it says will help us in those times: Ephesians 3:16-19, 2 Samuel 22:30, Judges 16:28, Exodus 15:2, Philippians 4:13, Psalm 119:97-98 and Psalm 119:11.

PRAYER OF REPENTANCE OF UNRIGHTEOUS RELATIONSHIPS

Lord, please strengthen me and give me wisdom to manage my affections and attractions. You have been with me through all the choices I have made, good and bad. For that, I am grateful. During the past (or present) times, when I have felt drawn to a relationship that does not please You, I realise that yielding to these temptations is sinful. For this, I repent, Lord.

Please help me to see the bigger picture. Give me a new level of wisdom in managing my attractions. Help me to see the root of my heart's desires and uproot the parts of me that are deceived. Fill my need for affection and admiration through Your Word and through the body of Christ. Remind me, Lord, that I am Your princess daughter, and You will only send me a spouse who belongs to You as well, and who is able to cover the strong calling on my life.

Protect me from being tricked by the enemy. Help me to discern counterfeits who may come my way. Empower me to break the cycle of giving my attention to unsaved persons. Let my mind and heart stay focused on You, Jesus. Amen.

PRAYER WHEN THERE IS ANGER TOWARDS GOD

Father, I have held on to offence against You. It has forged distance in my relationship with You, which may have given way to added affliction in my life. I choose to confess that I believed a lie about You. I acknowledge that this action, even if born out of my disappointment, is sinful towards You. I ask You, God, to forgive me. Give me a clear and accurate understanding of where the blame belongs. I receive the truth of Your Word and character that You love me, and Your goodness and mercy follow me all the days of my life.

When suffering comes and I feel bewildered, help me remember and truly believe I am never alone. Heal my heart and mend my relationship with You, free of unforgiveness, in Jesus' name. Amen.

Chapter 2

I Am Spoken For

"For the angel of the Lord is a guard; he surrounds and defends all who fear Him." (Psalm 34:7 – NLT).

If there is one recurring experience I have had throughout my life from a young age, it is being in a position where I felt like I was being challenged to prove my worth. When attending choir practice at my prep school, I was late because of my parents, resulting in me being treated 'differently' and even being punished by my teachers. When put in the "always late" category, a child in my shoes easily felt disliked and dismissed. In choir practice, however, my talent was hard to dismiss, especially at that age when the big, melodious sound coming from me did not match my size. Still, I was not the only child in the choir who sang beautifully, and there were certainly more 'suited' children who never arrived late, who held the favour of the choir mistress, and others who simply had a voice that effortlessly shunned. From this age, I began to learn that in this world, I would not always be given a fair chance, not even by those expected to be impartial, and that I could either allow myself to be dismissed or I could refuse to go unseen and "prove my worth." The odds were against me, even if I was too young to understand what they were and why, but deep down inside, I felt it.

My mother was a fierce defender of her children, not in the way of condoning wrongdoings but in the way that if her children were being ill-treated in any way by anyone, she would make it a duty to promptly confront and address it. For example, after dropping off my brother inside his fifth-grade classroom one morning, she happened to overhear his teacher accosting him in his class using words that she believed had been damaging to her son. My mother immediately returned to the classroom, said nothing, and took him out of the class. In one clean sweep, she decided right then and there to extricate him and our younger brother, who was also attending the institution. The incident had been one too many, and my mother did not need another to confirm what she had already sensed: the environment was not good for her child. She did not see the benefit in subjecting her boys to such experiences, and since I had already left and was in high school by this time, Mom was prepared to cut the ties.

Some may not agree with her approach, and perhaps it could have been handled differently, but one thing that experience taught us about our mother is that we could count on her to have our backs, to defend us, knowing that she was not one to stand idly by while we faced maltreatment. This increased our respect for her and amplified our self-confidence and resolve to do the same for ourselves and others.

Nevertheless, in moments when I did not have my mother physically there to do the job, the experience of "having to prove my worth" would come up at several intervals on small and large scales. In high school, when I decided to run for the position of head girl, I remember the opposition I received from a few student voters who did not deem me a suitable representative for student leadership because they had seen me at parties—the same parties they obviously also attended for them to enjoy without consequence, but for an aspiring head girl, it was to be held against her. I guess a reason had to be found to support their position despite my level of involvement and track record of student leadership from the moment I entered high school. In the end, I lost the race to head girl but was voted as one of the deputies, which I regarded as an honour nonetheless.

There was also the time when I entered the Miss Jamaica World pageant, which had a series of mini-competitions called fast track competitions, one of which was for the most talented. I knew I wanted to do a musical theatre piece because it would allow me to sing, act, and even do a little dancing or movement. I decided on "I Could Have Danced All Night" from "My Fair Lady," written by Andrew Lloyd Webber. Even though I knew the song very well, I wanted to make sure I would give the performance my utmost best, so I booked a session with a renowned voice trainer, vocalist, and dear friend I frequently sang with at concerts—the great

Carole Reid. With the voice of an angel, her bellowing high soprano voice had a reputation for arresting audiences. Our session helped me to master some technical maneuvering of my voice while adding an extra ounce of pzazz to top off the performance.

On the day of the talent competition, I eagerly awaited my turn to hit the stage which was in a spacious room with a table of about four judges encircled by a room of nervous beauty-queen hopefuls. My time came; I stood before the judges and began my performance, singing and moving across the room as I had practiced. Before reaching the halfway mark of the performance, I was startled by the voice of the competition's chief organiser at the time: *"No, no, stop! Lip syncing is not allowed."* As he commanded, I stopped performing, feeling befuddled and frightened, believing that I had somehow jeopardised myself. By the time he repeated his statements, my senses returned, and I soberly responded, *"Sir, I am not lip-syncing."* Above the judges who were appointed to govern the talent competition, the organiser was blatantly and publicly accusing me of pretending to sing and commanding me to cease. My fellow contenders in the room were silent, shocked at what was happening. I asked if I could restart my piece without the music to "prove" that I, in fact, was not lip-syncing, partially because of the first and secondhand embarrassment I felt but also because I still wanted to continue in the competition after all. Furthermore, I thought this was kind of a compliment, as untoward as the experience was, to have sounded so good that someone thought it was a track. My confidence was bolstered, and I performed my piece again, followed by a round of applause and even a standing ovation from some in the room. I won the talent competition, whether that was because it was duly earned or because the organisation felt compelled to award me after the cringe-worthy ordeal. Either way, here it was again, another instance of proving my worth and, this time, doing so in front of an audience.

There were private instances of the same, and the most vivid example was with the mother of a past boyfriend. From the start, she seemed to have decided on a (op)position against my presence in her son's life, and she was sure to let it be known. But prior to that, I remember the anticipation I had of meeting the family of the young man I had been so impressed with; how I began to envision what outfit I would wear to convey my warm personality and how we would engage in conversation about my background and my ambitions. To my dismay, the initial meeting was barely an introduction as I can recall us arriving and my then-boyfriend walking far ahead of me into his house on that fateful weeknight. I trailed behind him as he entered and gave a lackluster outburst alerting people there of his arrival, and then, if my memory serves well, he casually said, "This is Stephanie"—not with any real purpose or careful consideration. This was, at least, what the experience felt like for me. In response, I hardly remember his mother—who might have been otherwise occupied—acknowledging the introduction, not that she had been given the best opportunity to do so since it had been so run-of-the-mill; she simply responded in like fashion. That first interaction set the tone for the duration of the year plus of that relationship. I spent the entire time feeling like I was unseen and unimportant, particularly by this mother. There was little to no communication between us, especially when my boyfriend went overseas to work and live, which further reduced my chances of "proving my worth" amidst clear displays of disapproval and the poor view that was held of me and my family, reportedly. In this instance, not only was I viewed and treated as unworthy, but so was my family.

The experience was a pivotal one in my life, and it would take God's patience and healing to bring me to a place of forgiveness and insight into the darkness of the human heart, at times even that of those who claim to be followers of Christ.

I wasn't raised with a real appreciation of the concept of "Asking daddy's permission." My dad took a laissez-faire approach to fathering us, you know, not really getting involved in the nitty gritty. Though present in our lives, his method was a hands-off kind of approach.

As my parents' marriage deteriorated, my relationship with my father gradually crumbled into obscurity. His presence in the details of my life increasingly became like a shadow and was sadly more mechanical than anything else. Between needing lunch money for school and a ride somewhere, those became the extent to which we had conversations. His voice seemed to have very little to no bearing on my regular decision-making and life occurrences. Eventually, I would just do my own thing, and when I became an adult, that only intensified, along with my resentment.

After being convinced that my father was decidedly unattached, unavailable, and disinterested in the details of my life affairs, there was very little anybody could say to cause me to feel positively towards him. The truth is that even if none of what I thought was true, the limited communication between us that characterised the relationship did not make things any better. By this time, my walls had been raised higher than he could reach, even if he tried. In order to not feel the pain of the situation, I made myself completely emotionally inaccessible to him, tired of what felt like the most painful of all the experiences of having to "prove my worth." I had stored up enough indifference to stave off any kind of input from him, and I felt no remorse because any sign of that would mean weakness, and I was fixated on showing my strength and independence as a retaliation for his absence.

This rebellious tendency towards my father's authority was not something I was entirely conscious of, nor did I realise how my mother's disdain due to her poor experiences with him had such an influence on me, worse since I did not have my own personal bond with him. Little did I know, this would later have dire implications on my relationships with pretty much all the men who would enter my life.

From male bosses and male friends to love interests, the relationship I had with my father had in some way framed the manner in which I engaged with the opposite sex and the expectations I had, informed by my deep yearning for validation and male affection, that is, a masculine presence a girl needs who she can trust to affirm her when needed with no ulterior motives. My deep longings and lack of awareness thereof only left me vulnerable and slightly desperate.

When I would meet a guy I liked, my procedures were simple: see guy, like guy, flirt with guy, wait for guy to approach, and get with guy. Simple. I was a simple girl who did not need the games and mystery, nor did I seem inclined towards a lengthy getting-to-know-you process. I did not practice taking time to observe uncomfortable things like self-control and patience and asking hard questions at the risk of offending or making things awkward. I pretty much allowed the tide of "good vibes" to carry me wherever it wished—and carry me it did. I swayed from encounter to encounter with guys from backgrounds, beliefs, and values very far from mine but guys who I was attracted to, whether for their good looks, charm, 'swag,' the excitement, or the thrill of them being from a different world. From the unashamed hedonistic boyfriends to the militantly devout Christian perceived as the perfect saint; from a divorcee who I learned was horrendously abusive, to a multi-millionaire Brit who was determined—and I mean DETERMINED—to sweep me off my feet, out of my country and into his lavish home to be with him, his children—and his children's mother. When I think of these things, I recall the colourful journey my life has been, and I feel ever more grateful for the hand of my heavenly Father in every chapter.

By the time I finally had enough of being broken-hearted from failed romantic relationships, mostly as a result of my misguided decisions, I cried out to God, asking "Why do I keep doing this? Why do I always end up here?" His answer would astound me. It was a clear, divine response that brought tremendous understanding.

I learned that because of my 'wild child,' orphan-like mindset (think Peter Pan) of independently making decisions, especially around matters of the heart, without seeking counsel, without "asking permission," I continually landed in situations that ended in regret. Because I had so practiced being the daughter who thought she was beyond asking permission, that behaviour spilled over into my relationship with God. I realised because of what had been my norm for so many years, believe it or not, I just did not know how to be a 'good daughter.' I had to learn how to accept that I was spoken for, I belonged to Someone, and even if my earthly dad did not do everything he could to actively claim his role in my life, I still had a heavenly Father who had made Himself evident beyond the shadow of a doubt. The time had come for me to acknowledge this truth, agree that I had been wrong, ask for forgiveness, submit to Him, and turn around my behaviour. At twenty-something, I had to start seeing myself as Daddy's little girl and ask His permission.

In the book, *Overcoming Father Wounds: Exchanging Your Pain For God's Perfect Love (Chapter 8),* the author, Kia Stephens, asserts that there are noticeable responses based on different approaches to fathering. The roles our earthly fathers play directly affect our view of and relationship with our heavenly Father. Authoritarian fathers can lead to their children rebelling against God; abusive fathers can cause their children to have difficulty trusting, being vulnerable with, and emotionally relating to God; distant and passive fathers can cause their children to view God as uninvolved and disinterested in their life (this description applied to my experience), and absent fathers can cause their children to view God as inaccessible or non-existent.

The book's message resonates with what I have been coming to terms with over the years: *"the void of the father-wounded daughter is filled (only) with the infinite love of God."*

As much as I desired a deeper connection with my dad, which I only became personally aware of in my adulthood, the truth is, I do have experiences where I depended on him, and he was there for me. I can remember in my teenage years of party-going, I could rely on my father to be a sure ride to and after an event. In hindsight, it was a chance for him to see for himself where I was going for entertainment and get a sense of who I was there with. He occasionally exercised some paternal instinct by expressing disapproval of my scantily clad party attire. All of which I took for granted then, admittedly. I would brush him off and carry on with my friends, and later in the night, if I could not secure a ride home, I knew I could call him to pick me up, even if it was 3:00 am. Of course, there were times when I did not want to bother him at those odd hours, and there were times when I did not necessarily want to wait the additional time it would take for him to (wake up fully), get ready, and come for me.

As I have come closer to understanding the character and heart of God towards me, I see similarities between both (God and my father) reflecting on this memory. How much of a picture it is of duty and responsibility in love. Isn't it like God to show up for us in our hour of need, no questions asked? Especially from those messy situations we have somehow managed to get ourselves in. He comes when we call, and even if we have to wait or if He shows up in a way unlike one we envisioned, the bottom line is that He shows up. He is dependable. Without giving my father the credit he deserved, I guess you could say I felt confident that he would show up when I really needed him to, and all I needed to do was ask.

Let's face it: no one likes to ask for what they want, especially if that thing is more affection. *May I have more affection, please?* It does not exactly roll off the tongue. Even worse, if you are not self-aware enough to realise and be able to verbalise that that is, in fact, what you want. I have seen it in myself as I have grown older, so much I do not even recognise what I am longing for until someone helps me see it. After recognizing, the process of being vulnerable and sharing that with whomever you desire it from can be even harder.

Sometimes, depending on the person's personality, general nature, stage of emotional intelligence, and other factors, we may find this even more difficult as we begin to anticipate what their response will be, which is, in our minds, often unfavourable.

Take, for instance, the time I told an older woman, who was one of my mentors and Bible Study leaders, that I was involved in a sexual relationship at the time with an older man and I felt guilty about it. I shared that I felt unworthy of serving in ministry, considering I was assigned leadership roles, and I remember even asking her if she thought God still deemed me suitable to serve His people. Her answer was simple and loving. She said, *"Stephanie, you need your father."* It was clear to me that the answer implied I needed to go before the heavenly Father, but it was also clear that she was referring to my earthly father too.

By now, I had been somewhat aware of the impact of not having a close relationship with my dad. Still, apart from writing a letter of forgiveness to him, which he might have received in utter confusion, I did not really know what other steps I needed to take to heal from this *brokenness* I was feeling. I have learned that writing a letter of forgiveness also requires you to ask them for forgiveness—an important part I left out—which, in hindsight, may have made a difference in my father's response. In any case, what do you do when your father is alive and well but just emotionally unavailable, seemingly preoccupied with other things without ever really expressing, verbally or otherwise, a desire for closeness? It is perplexing to maneuver as it is painful, especially because you have no choice but to accept that the circumstances may never change. Thankfully, the Lord graciously held my hand and directed me to Him so I could be equipped and strengthened for the journey ahead.

With the reassurance I received from my mentor, I felt confident that I was more than worthy, and with a repentant heart and the ability to make different choices, I could be restored. I went forward, one step at a time, being faithful with whatever task I was called to at that time, and slowly began to see my heart heal. One of the impactful conversations that helped me shift my perspective towards my father and, subsequently, my perspective on our relationship was with one of my uncles, who gave me a window into what my father was like growing up. *"Let's just say, if I don't call your father, I know I won't hear from him,"* he said, and at the same moment, it was disappointing as well as comforting. My father has never been one to make a great effort to maintain familial relationships, and it was not just with me; it was with everyone. I guess that meant I did not need to take it so personally, but still, it bothered me, and I figured there was much more to his background and why he was the way he was. It was not to be seen as an excuse but as insight.

I believe many of us are facing or have faced situations like these with parents, primary caregivers, or other members of our families. I have a close friend whose mother grew up being treated as an "outcast" by her mother and, in return, was abusive verbally towards her—my friend—throughout her childhood and even in adulthood. Their relationship is rife with deep hurt, bitterness, and constant arguing, though the love between them is also undeniable. No doubt, in a situation like this, there is a great need for healthy boundaries and heart-repair from the Physician Himself while we do the work of forgiveness and seek well-needed affirmation in Christ, that is, through prayer and reading the Word that bears the truth of who we are in the eyes of our God. It is important to bear this point in mind because the reality is that if we have been raised without healthy, godly affirmation, then it is unlikely that we will instinctively know how to rightfully affirm ourselves. We cannot give to ourselves what we have never received or have been exposed to. What we need exists outside of ourselves. What we need is the love of our Saviour. Without addressing the voids in our lives that have existed since childhood, we risk not being able to trust people, constantly seeking validation from relationships to no avail, and experiencing deeper emptiness that can feel impossible to fill. A book called "Mother Hunger" by trauma counsellor, Kelly McDaniel, refers to that void, comparing it to a lack of nurturance, protection, and guidance and the impact it can have on daughters. It explores the patterns that often form, including a trail of unstable and painful relationships and insatiable desire for sex and love, often viewed as the same thing. She highlights that instead of constantly searching for love to fill that void, the journey to healing begins with recognising our behavioural patterns and coming into knowing and naming what we are missing.

A SECRET WISH

It's a thought that brings tears to my eyes.
The picture of a girl
Holding her daddy's hand
Firm and directive, as he leads
She looks up at him; his steps guide her path
Somewhere midway, he lifts her in the air
And the two are inseparable.

Late night heartbreak stories
She freely shares while he listens intently
And reassures her of her worth
His precious jewel, the apple of his eye
His words and embrace of protection
Gives her all the shielding from a cold world
And when age has crept upon them
She still leans on his shoulder
And the familiar assurance she will find
Even when his hands tremble and eyes fall
No new love will ever replace his
Her daddy, always and forever hers.
And yet, I find myself in tears
For the beautiful thought remains just that
Will it ever be more, I wonder.
More than a thought.
A secret wish.

AIR HUG

I wish I could feel your embrace
Wrap myself in Your arms
Feel your shelter from harm,
Filled with the warmth of your love.

When all the world is against me
And I feel all alone
When my heart is sad and weary
And your word is all I can stand on.

I wish I could feel your embrace
Wrap myself in Your arms
Feel your shelter from harm,
Filled with the warmth of your love.

I wish I could lay my head
Lay it against your chest
Be held so tenderly
Yet firmly protected.

Like a daddy holds his daughter
Wipes the tears from her face
I can trust that in the darkness
You will be my Light.

In the face of life's troubled days
To your arms I will run
And you will hold me near

I wish I could feel your embrace
Wrap myself in Your arms
Feel your shelter from harm,
Filled with the warmth of your love.

Rest, I wanna rest
Rest in Your arms, Lord.

STRONG MAN

I want you to hold me.
Embrace me.
Let me feel masculine hands
Engulf my entire being.
Surround me with warmth
As I rest my head on your bosom.

Your scent is my refuge
My face buried in your shirt.
Strong, manly fingers unbreakable
Discover the small of my back.
All inhibitions and fears are lost

As I escape to your arms.
Eyes closed tight,
Tiny hands no longer clenched with fright;
My whimper screams
Don't let me go.
Please, don't let me go.

PERSONAL REFLECTIONS

1. Do you know what it feels like to be disappointed or let down by someone you care for deeply? It could be a friend, a romantic interest, or a family member. Describe it here.

2. After the incident, what was your attitude towards that person and to others?

3. The poem "A Secret Wish" is about a young girl's wish for her relationship with her father. How relatable is this poem for you, if at all?

4. Write down any secret wishes you may have for your relationship with a family member/s who has/have hurt you. If this activity is deeply painful for you, then pause and say the prayer titled Prayer During Emotional Pain at the end of Chapter 2.

5. What are the top three things you appreciate about your relationship with God, your heavenly Father?

6. Have you ever felt like you expected something from God and He did not deliver? Write about it here, maybe in a poem form if you are so inclined. If you have unforgiveness towards God, say the prayer titled

"Prayer When There Is Anger Towards God" at the end of Chapter 1.

PRAYER DURING EMOTIONAL PAIN

God, the pain I feel cannot be put into words. I feel alone and bewildered. I am crying out to You and begging for some relief. Please help me to process these feelings. You have seen how long this has been a struggle. Perform the spiritual surgery on my heart that is needed to help me become whole. I have operated from the broken place, whether or not I have been conscious of it, and I want that to change as of this moment. Show me the roots of unforgiveness that have tied me to this pain and turned me into a slave. By Your grace, I release and choose to forgive _____, even as I acknowledge Your Spirit as my Comforter, from the pain they caused me. I pray as of today, only love will flow from my heart as I glorify You now and always. Amen.

Chapter 3

An Audit of the Heart

broken/ˈbrəʊk(ə)n/ *past participle of break;* having breaks or gaps in continuity.

I am from a broken family unit. I believe my family has been "broken" from its inception. When my mother and father married, they had different world views, held different values, and, as young twenty-somethings, potentially lacked a complete knowledge of themselves and of each other—not much different from many other couples. I suspect that when my mother became pregnant with me, while being a member of her local church and unmarried, she may have decided it was the "proper" thing to marry the man she had shared this milestone with, despite clear differences in beliefs, interests, and almost everything else. To add to this, my mother had come out of a long-term relationship prior to my father, which she thought would have led to marriage, but things took a different turn. She may have decided to earnestly hope for my father to eventually share her spiritual convictions and that he would love her deeply since he came from what appeared to her as an exemplary family unit with both parents in the home. Meanwhile, my father might not have been clear on what he was signing up for, and the level of self-sacrifice and commitment marriage would require of him. The circumstances led to a less-than-ideal start to a future together. In reality, any kind of shaky foundation will most likely lead to a shaky structure and, ultimately, the frail structure will break.

Coming to terms with this has not been easy for me, even though it was clear that I had no control over the circumstances I was born into. Still, these realisations can come with the alleged stages of grief: denial, anger, bargaining, depression, and then acceptance. There was a time I battled bitterness towards my parents, thinking about how their decisions affected my present life and made me into the "mess" that I was. *It was their fault.* Being the eldest gave me no respite in our household as I did not really have anyone around paying attention to the pain I was feeling on account of the challenges in our household. What was the result? A little girl who developed a deep lack of trust for those in authority and believed it was her duty to fend for herself and protect her younger siblings. This resentment would manifest more in adulthood in the form of ongoing disputes between my parents and me.

I remember a particular season of life when I had different ideas from them on my career choices. I went through a year of unemployment and refused to pursue a job just for the sake of having one, but instead, I chose to take some time to hear from God and plan my next steps toward a more purposeful and fulfilling livelihood. Of course, I made this decision while living rent-free at about twenty-five years old in the house they raised me in. I was privileged to have been in this position. I was still contributing towards bills, but it was to a lesser degree than before because I was jobless, and my parents were less than amused. I remember my mother believing that I surely had a mental breakdown. It was one of the few times my parents agreed and sang the same tune, and I did not care to hear it. The truth is, maybe I was experiencing a form of emotional or mental breakdown during that time due to a number of factors. Add to that the combination of not knowing how to cry out to them for help and feeling pressured as their firstborn, who they had expected so much from. It was just an overall painful ordeal. This was new terrain for all of us, and we were not managing well.

God had been present in all of this. When I look back, I believe He allowed us to get to the point of harsh words being spewed, raw emotions expressed, and bitterness surfacing from their crevices as a purification, and it was a messy one. When a wound is infected, it sometimes has to be squeezed to properly treat and heal (a strange analogy, but it's the best one I have). It was also during this time that God presented Himself to me vividly as the *One who held my purpose.* I cried out to Him in desperation, broken as ever, and He spoke. For four days consecutively, I woke up to meet with Him at the same time, and my aim was to *Ask, Seek and Knock.* More than ever before, I needed clarity on my purpose, and I was not going to stop asking until He answered. God faithfully did just that and gave me visuals and words that came in the form of a constant stream of thoughts. I struggled to write it all down because the thoughts were flowing like a flood. This was also how I knew they were not my own, but they were from a source external to me. He told me that I would build a fortress for His people where they would receive living water, and He said I would not build it on my own but with the husband He would send me. *Hold up, God! Husband?* I was not prepared for that part of the pursuit for purpose, but I had to admit, I was intrigued. When I asked God to tell me more about this husband, what I gleaned again was clear:

"He will come from a foreign land."
"He will adore you; he will see you as gold."
"His family will love you."
"When you meet, you will know."
"He will be able to tell you the details of your purpose."

Two years after I had this exchange with God, and interestingly, the year I first met the man who is now my husband, we revisited the conversation, and God clarified even further:

"Though he comes from a foreign land, I did not say he was a foreigner."

"He will be a breath of fresh air, not carrying the same insecurities as some of the men from before, and you will be the same for him."

This clarification was crucial as my original interpretation led me to believe that my husband was not Jamaican like me. I mean, when you hear, "He comes from a foreign land," it is reasonable to assume he is a foreigner. However, God happens to be the Master of mystery while being completely clear and unambiguous. He means what He says, and He says what He means. God has no difficulty articulating or expressing thought like we do. As you read on, you will see what I mean.

Before I delve into the revelations mentioned above, there is an important lesson I want to underscore. If you believe you have heard from God, do not doubt it, but ensure that you hold it loosely enough in case you misinterpreted what God meant. Sometimes what we have heard or sensed is correct, but how we interpret what we have heard may not be entirely correct. The beauty of God is that if we are ever incorrect about anything, He is willing and able to clarify what He means. All we need to do is remain open and be very prayerful before taking any kind of action.

For example, I recall a time when a close friend of mine, Kayla, and I were praying together, insistent on asking God directly about a man I had been engaging with. Upon her insisting, we decided to ask God if he was my husband. As we prayed, asking, seeking, and knocking for a response from the

Lord, she saw a vision of me in a wedding gown, twirling and laughing happily. As she shared, my immediate interpretation was that God was saying this man IS my husband! I contained my thoughts and excitement. Shortly after that, as we continued to pray, my friend spoke words that I believe were directly from God Himself. She said, *"You are Mine. Do not throw your pearls to swine."* My friend may not have known how I initially interpreted the vision she had seen, but God knew, and He chose to clarify in a most loving and equally terrifying way. Many more things were said that evening that made it clear that this man was not going to be my husband. I left that experience very sure that God's love for me was protective and He was not going to allow His daughter to be swept away by any counterfeits.

My purpose being revealed to me during the course of those four days would serve as my guiding light for years to come. It was the answer I needed for how I would re-enter the work world, my measuring stick for the associations I needed to form, and my guide in how I would respond to men who were interested in me. It made me appreciate the importance of God's consistent involvement in our lives. Navigating life without Him is truly the definition of walking blind. I knew I would need to work in spaces that encourage creativity and serve people's needs for personal and professional growth, and when I became aware of this, doors opened.

I resumed work with a company that sought to improve sales development within organisations, offering training to sales professionals. This experience gave me the confidence to embark on the role of being a part-time trainer, delivering a program I designed for young professionals on "Corporate Deportment." Who would have thought that the person who, only a year ago, had been jobless for almost a year would now be training people on how to keep their jobs and do well in them? From experience, I had known the importance of learning self-management skills and the effects of poor professionalism. I had experienced suffering under the weight of poor leadership in the companies I had worked for and took away a few learning points to ensure that I became a leader with integrity. I was more than prepared to help build certain skills in people who were just like me to help them have a more enriching experience in the workplace.

As far as associations that I needed to form, I realised it was important for me to build relationships with persons who were driven and making an impact in shared areas of interest. I joined a global network of young professionals who were aspiring change-makers simply because I needed to learn how they achieved their goals. I craved their insight, and there was the added benefit of being able to air things and exchange ideas on things that mattered to me in a space where those around me would understand. They knew what it was like to feel a sense of purpose and an insatiable desire for things like social impact. The Global Shapers Kingston Hub not only put me in the company of new colleagues who would become a new family that shared my passions and even sense of patriotism, but I found myself faced with opportunities to visit other countries and build those same bonds with persons from the opposite end of the world. The reality of it is still hard to fathom. To think that I had only just begun the pursuit of what I now understand as my purpose, and here I was, stepping into it accompanied by inspiring individuals from all over the world.

I was in awe of God.

My life had taken a turn for the better in many ways, and I found that I was doing much better emotionally and mentally, even making wiser decisions in the love-life department. I almost did not realise that I had gone a couple of years without the thought of liking a boy. No dating or secret admiring, nothing. I was finally detached from any romantic interests, completely single, and able to focus on my personal growth. Of course, my revelation of the husband from "a foreign land" also played a role and caused me to only have eyes for one who was from abroad initially. This ruled out a few Jamaican guys who had expressed interest, as you can imagine, but as much as my interpretation of God's message had been flawed, it almost seemed like He allowed me to keep believing that for a while as some form of protection. In any case, once I knew a husband would come along eventually, I naturally made no real effort trying to find him. My attention was otherwise engaged. I was completely smitten by the thought of more travel, and the further from home I went, the more fascinated I was. I was intrigued by the countries that were further away because of the vastly different cultures and unmatched hospitality.

My first trip with the Global Shapers Community was to China. It was a most unexpected place for me as I had no real desire initially, but an opportunity was extended, and I could not find a reason not to grab it. I am so happy that I did. That trip afforded me a stopover in South Korea, and although I was only there for a few hours, the thought of traversing through these different territories excited me. These travels also gave me a taste of the respective places and made me want to return. My experience in China provided me with friendships I still treasure today, but perhaps the greatest gain can only be explained as "an unlocking." There are reserves in our minds, I believe, that do not become activated or stimulated until we have had certain experiences. I believe travel is one such experience—to be immersed in another country, even if only for a few days, walk their streets, eat their food, inhale their signature scents, listen to the variety of sounds from people chattering in local dialects to authentic music, and feel the spirit of a new people group while observing how much more you have in common than not. All of this adds a certain quality to living, enabling us to empathise and truly be human.

I did not realise it then, but travel had been a gift that God gave me to aid in my healing process. The wonders of travelling to far places alone and navigating that experience with God as my only companion is inexplicable. Make no mistake, the experience often involves some anxiety, fear, worry, and other uncomfortable feelings, but even those moments are opportunities to learn more about ourselves and, more importantly, experience God personally and directly.

The year after my trip to China, I visited Bangladesh, with flight stopovers in Italy and Dubai, where I spent the night in an airport hotel because of a very long layover. I also travelled to Thailand. I had company for part of the journey through a good friend and fellow Jamaican Global Shaper. I travelled to Switzerland, and that extended to leisure trips to France and Germany. Two years of visiting countries that were no less than a 10-hour flight away opened my eyes greatly and served my need for healing in ways that continue to be revealed.

At different stages of my life, I believe God intervened and brought me different measures of healing. I can recall the intervention that resulted in my developing a strong desire to learn the Word during times of Bible Study with sisters in Christ who were from different backgrounds, of varying ages, and from different churches. These women became my sisters through and through and demonstrated the love of Christ to me in the time and counsel they lovingly offered me. Being immersed in an environment like this allows you to feel comfortable and loved and lends itself to vulnerability and trust, which can result in becoming more aware of things that hold no prominence in your mind.

After sharing about family backgrounds, heartbreak, challenges at work, areas of 'lack,' battles with illness, it is inevitable that we would find ourselves questioning things—

sensitive parts of us that had been neglected—as well as realising just how much Jesus had redeemed us from. For example, generational patterns that are undeniably active in our lives, both blessings and curses, you begin to feel the veil literally lift from your eyes. But with all this information coming at you, it can be overwhelming if we make the mistake of taking our eyes off Christ as the scales are being removed.

I have gone back and forth from sinking under and floating above the weight of the revelations God has given me. Still, for every retreat, 'encounter weekend,' conference, healing ministry, etc., that I have engaged in, God graciously used those settings to bring me closer to Him to see more clearly how much I needed Christ to heal me.

A few of those revelations have been grandiose and unfathomable, while others have been simple yet profound. There was a time God revealed to me that the enemy had been after my self-esteem from the time I was in my mother's womb. Possibly bearing the guilt and shame of being pregnant out of wedlock and thereby facing excommunication for a brief time from her local church, my mother might have passed on these emotions to her unborn child. My mother had never shared with me how she felt in that year of her pregnancy with me, yet God saw it fit to reveal her emotions at that time to me. When I think about it, it is incredible that God would want so badly for me to know how to pray and what to uproot to help me break chains that the enemy would have sought to keep me bound by. I do recall, throughout my life, especially in childhood, struggling with healthy self-esteem, and that manifested in several ways as I got older, but it mostly took the form of a prevailing feeling of not being good enough. That revelation was the start of the turning point that would cause me to look more inwardly and peer into the things that are unseen, like the history of my family members, the unspoken and uncomfortable events of the past, and the operation of good and bad spirits in my life. I became vested in understanding how I was wired and the 'why' behind all my actions.

I spent a year pursuing a course in layman's counselling led by someone who was a certified psychologist but also one who I regarded as a Christian spiritual mother, and the experience was so powerful that it led me to address my own needs for counselling. Added to that, I had heard a teaching by a preacher who revealed statistics on the detrimental effects of divorce on children based on a particular study. The findings of the research were astounding. I was so taken with the findings that I went online and scoured the study "The Unexpected Legacy of Divorce." It was a twenty-five-year-long study of 131 children whose parents divorced when they were between the ages of 3-18 years old. At the 25-year mark, the research included a comparison group of their peers from the same community. The disparities were evident between those growing up intact versus divorced/separated families, but the most alarming finding to me was the challenges that nearly all the children of divorce found in having healthy perspectives and experiences in love, sexual intimacy, marriage, and parenthood.

This sobered me almost instantly, and in no time, I was booking my first appointment with a Christian-based counselling service. On the day of my first session, I was given a form to complete. I saw the term "Divorce" as one of the reasons for seeking counselling. It felt very strange as I ticked the option. All along, I thought my parents' divorce was their problem, yet somehow, I was there seeking counselling on account of their decisions, which were totally outside of my control; how absurd. But the reality was that their decisions did affect me, and it was a life lesson on the far-reaching effects of our sins as people. While I knew this in theory, I was only just coming to terms with it in a real way.

The first step was to acknowledge it. I was twenty-eight years old and just seeing the need for counselling after what had been years of a broken marriage between my primary caregivers. I was prepared to take on everything that came with that healing journey.

After a couple of years in the process, I decided to take things to another dimension. With my life's purpose seeming to be shaped around helping people to truly receive the inner healing and freedom that Jesus offers, I knew I needed to get as close as possible to that personally. It would be an ongoing process, but I wanted to see what was in store. Yes, I had been saved, as the Bible describes it, a work that happens once and lasts forever, thanks be to God, but the road to being free and staying that way was continuous. One too many conflicts with my parents left me feeling like all my deep wounds had been stepped on, and I realised I still needed more intervention.

Counselling had helped me unearth deep-rooted issues, and I could connect dots, which was an important step, but the time had come for even more.

As a trainee to become a facilitator in an inner healing and deliverance ministry known as Restoring the Foundations, I first had to become a recipient, and I decided to focus on freedom from my struggle with suppression of emotions and despondency. Those seemed like "simple" enough issues to address, but the truth is, I was in for much more than I had imagined. Part of the ministry allows the recipient to go through a process of addressing soul/spirit hurts where the recipient asks Jesus to reveal a memory of the source of the original hurt, and after the necessary confession of sin, forgiveness, releasing and renouncing, He reveals the root, and then He heals.

For both healing areas, Jesus appeared as we waited in prayer for Him to answer. In the case of despondency, I saw a visual of myself at three years old, walking down a driveway with my father, who held my hand. Then, he released my hand and went into his car to go and play tennis. I began to cry in the memory as well as tears fell from my face in real life even as my eyes were closed. I wrongfully came to the conclusion in the memory that I was not worth staying for. At that moment, Jesus entered. He took my father's place and held my hand instead of him. I looked up yearningly, and He looked down reassuringly, and I instantly felt better. Christ had made Himself present in a moment from my past, which I had no recollection of, but in this divine memory, He was showing that even if my father had left at that moment, I was not abandoned, nor was I alone then or now. Jesus thought I was worth staying for.

In the other memory, addressing the soul/spirit hurts from neglected and suppressed emotions, I recall myself standing behind a kitchen sink washing dishes while looking out through a window at a younger version of myself cartwheeling on a sloped lawn enclosed in a picket fence. The child version of myself was free and happily playing alone but completely unbothered, openly and joyfully expressing herself. My thoughts as I watched from the kitchen sink were two-fold: I wished I felt as free as the child on the lawn, and at the same time, I was concerned for her safety and almost sure that she would get hurt. The next thing I remember is Jesus appearing, again beside me, also looking out on the happy child. His presence was calming and soothing, though no words were exchanged, nor did we look at each other this time. My thoughts began to change towards the child. I knew that she was safe, and I began to celebrate internally her freedom as I looked on.

I cannot fully describe in words what this experience did for me, and perhaps only those who have experienced anything like it can understand. Since then, I have reaffirmed myself with truths that have replaced my ungodly beliefs. The work is ongoing, but more than anything else, I am grateful for what it has done for my faith and hope in Christ.

One thing I can say for sure is that Christ has and continues to pursue me with a love unlike any other man in my life. He has so loved me that I have come to know without a shadow of a doubt that I am His prized possession. However, I did not always see myself in this light, and my decisions certainly did not always reflect this belief. Still, God has used my failings in romantic relationships to reveal Himself to me more than ever. It took me being completely shattered to have a longing, right heart toward Him.

When I think back to those times when my resolve to follow Jesus grew stronger, it makes my fondness for Him much more intense and His love for a wretch like me more evident. Isn't that what we all seek? We want to know that even in our most wretched states, in all the areas we fall short, someone will still love us so deeply, not simply tolerate us, nor be weirdly obsessed with us, but love us even when we fail at loving them.

So many times, I can remember just getting to know someone I was pursuing a romantic relationship with when neither of us could do anything wrong for the other. Infatuation has a way of clouding judgment, and then the fear of failure and disappointment also push people to live in denial and pretend that all is well when it is not. However, as time progresses, it becomes harder to turn a blind eye to that thing you always ignored even though it really bothered you, or it becomes that much more challenging to continue being the false person you have forced yourself to be in order to please your suitor—the truth begins to eventually rear its head. Now, the countdown begins as to how long the relationship will last.

I remember when I 'broke up' with a man who I was with for a few months. I initially had absolutely no interest in more than friendship, but a combination of being in a vulnerable state at that time (I had recently broken off something with a different person) and being relentlessly pursued by this new guy led me to give in and 'giving things a shot.' He spoke my love language. He was funny, entertaining, and controversial. We had stirring conversations, but in my heart of hearts, I knew he was a distraction—just the way he refused to take "No" for an answer when I told him I was not interested, showing he did not respect boundaries, the way he almost ridiculed me in my spiritual convictions calling me "Sister Steph" and the way our conversations, though engaging, hardly left me feeling edified. Yet, when he turned up in the audience of a play I was in and, at another time, insisted on accompanying me to a singing engagement at a resort out of town, then treating my mother to a beautiful lunch and bouquet of her favourite colour flowers for her birthday, I found myself eventually falling hard for him. Some things about him made me unsure, even if I had managed to have a complete turn of heart and admired almost every trait I thought I had observed. Everything came to a halt when things ended between us, and he demanded that I pay him back the money he had previously spent on a plane ticket so that I could go to New York with him. It was eye-opening, to say the least, and all the perfection that we had found in each other dissipated, and eventually, I saw everything for what it was.

LOVE, YOUR FATHER

The whole world is hurting
And yet, many do not bemoan
to Me.
They find many false ways of coping
Until they become blinded
Unable to perceive their pain.

But not you, my beloved.
You run to Me in your anguish
You cry out, arms outstretched
And I hear your call
I have cried with you
I feel your pain.

But I don't only feel it
I bear it today as I bore it at Calvary
Once and for all.
Run to Me, darling
I know how to carry this weight
And to Me, it's not heavy.

I have come that you may truly live
Freely and powerfully
Not as a victim or as spoiled goods.
But as My handy-work of art
I have thrown over you
A multi-coloured coat to show My favour.

No weapon formed against you
Will ever prosper.
As you stand firm in the protection
Of My favour and love
I define who you are
You are mine.

You allow yourself to feel hurt
As you crave an authentic relationship
For My glory.
I will protect you, love.
You are protected.
I will defend and provide for you.

PERSONAL REFLECTIONS

1. Can you recall ever feeling comforted by Christ's Spirit (The Holy Spirit) during a difficult time? Describe it here.

2. How do you handle yourself when you are experiencing pain? How do you express it?

3. How does knowing that God cries with you in your deepest times of anguish make you feel?

4. What do you think is the link between allowing ourselves to go through a painful ordeal (rather than pacifying it) and achieving authenticity in our relationships?

5. What do you think it means to have a heart that is not whole?

6. According to these scriptures, how do we acquire wholeness in our hearts and lives? (Joel 2:32, Psalm 139:14, Matthew 11:28-30, 2 Corinthians 3:17).

Chapter 4

The Rocky Road to Restored

"And the God of all grace, who called you to his eternal glory in Christ, after you have suffered a little while, will himself restore you and make you strong, firm and steadfast." (1 Peter 5:10 - NIV).

The thing about being on the road to a restored life is that it never happens seamlessly. There is always the occasional bump in the road, craters to derail you, and unexpected passers-by whose sole purpose is to distract you. I mentioned when I began attending Bible studies among women I admired greatly and shared the pleasure of walking alongside while growing in a knowledge of the Word. What I did not mention was that during the initial stages of that new journey, there were still areas of my life that needed intervention. While my love for Christ and devotion to Him had grown, I was still divided in my affections because of guys in my life who would never fit into the equation. I remember distinctly sobbing as I laid in bed one night, asking God what I had gotten myself into; this was in reference to a relationship I had entered into with a young man who was not a Christian but was someone I felt I had connected with. The circumstances had just seemed right for us to take things beyond friendship. I consciously denied what had been a cemented conviction and decided to press forward in an ungodly relationship.

I did this a couple of other times in those formative years of fellowshipping with my sisters, and I thank God that those who were aware never treated me with judgment but instead with grace, even while they persisted in seeing my life transform. There were countless one-on-one coffee dates, long chats and prayer times on living room couches and in parking lots, invitations to innumerable workshops, conferences, and encounter weekends that would impact my spiritual and personal development. I guess that was the key to my rocky road eventually smoothing out. Even without directly trying to "fix me," by simple association with these women who exemplified walking in faith and doing exploits for God's kingdom, I gained immeasurable strength that I needed to walk away from situations that were not serving me nor the purpose I was called to fulfil. Soon enough, I was victorious and made decisions that reflected that same victory, and eventually, I would have gotten to a place of imparting to others to help them do it too.

Although I had been experiencing victory, this did not mean the war taking place in the spirit realm had ceased. For those who are unaware, let me explain. Life as we know it exists in both physical and metaphysical or spiritual forms. There are the things we can see and those we cannot see, whether or not we believe they exist. I firmly believe what the Bible teaches about Satan being the enemy, the adversary, a roaring lion seeking whom he may devour, and I think we have all experienced in some way his unrelenting efforts to steal, kill, and destroy. But I believe even more that God is infinitely all-powerful and has no equal. I have seen that most of the time, when I am on a path that is good, there are people or circumstances that present themselves, and they turn out to be nothing more than obstacles. It was good that I was actively walking closer to God, but the vipers or "jackabites" (as my close friend Lisa calls demons) would still try their utmost best to deter me.

One example was in 2014, when I ushered in the year on the heels of a breakup. As if it wasn't bad enough that the person broke up with me; this happened right before Christmas. That year, I struggled with a profound anger that it felt like all the growth I had experienced in my Christian life leading up to that point did not mean much. I felt anger towards any man who professed Christianity, especially because this particular relationship had been my first one with a Christian, and in the end, I was left feeling disappointed and rejected. To be fair, the rejection came mostly from his family, who took a strong position against our being together, and they made their stance very clear. When we broke up, it felt like we had lost a battle and surrendered to them, giving them what they wanted from the beginning. The situation drove me to a place of disillusionment, and subsequently, I found myself in two very painful dating experiences that year while in a most vulnerable state. If we are not careful, the enemy can use our negative emotions as an open door to wreak even more havoc. This is why it is crucial to take time to heal from broken relationships before quickly moving on.

Many times, our coping mechanism for heartbreak is to avoid feeling the pain of rejection or avoid grieving the loss of a relationship and facing the reality of our own role in the mess. We do this by quickly moving on to the next candidate at the expense of true emotional and spiritual healing.

There was that time when I had been at a point of complete singleness, that is, not involved in any pseudo-relationships nor "talking" to a guy, no attachments to any previous boyfriends, no casual dating, no fantasising about anyone secretly. I was single and truly content. I had been preparing for my trip to China when I had a strange dream. I was clearly in a foreign place, and I was being led by a striking, tall man who wore what I can only describe as an adventurer's suit, complete with a backpack, safari hat, and industrial boots. He spoke with a British accent, held me firmly by the hand, and I was mesmerised. The next thing I remember is that we were in something like a cafeteria full of people around us. I sat on his lap, and somehow, our exchange became sexual while the group was being led in prayer. I remember uttering the words, "This is so wrong" before I woke up. Instantly, I knew the dream was meant to be a warning as I got ready to head to the conference in China.

When I arrived in China, literally at the airport, I met a man. He resembled the man in my dream—tall, dark, reminiscent of Idris Elba—and he spoke with a British accent. It stands to note that we were probably among the only black people in that space. It did not register at this point that my dream could have been referring to this person, even though the man had struck up a conversation and suggested that he wanted to see me again. I told myself I was not here to make romantic connections; I was focused on the conference and all that I had to learn, and I was interested in building my professional network. Even then, I could not help but be curious about the man. *Would I see him again?* Maybe I could find out about the presentation he told me he would be giving. I found myself becoming consumed with the thought of seeing this mystery man again who had left an impression and who had seemed to disappear after that first encounter. Lo and behold, when I finally decided to throw in the towel on the night of a cocktail event the group of us attended, I spotted him, and he, likewise, me. He made his way over to me, and we engaged in some cheeky banter as if we were long-time friends. "Oh, he lives," I remember was my opening statement, to which he responded with a smirk that showed a certain delight in my inquiring, and by the end of our tête-à-tête, he was holding my phone and saving his number. When I thought that would have been the end of our exchange that night, we bumped into each other a second time, and I found myself "whisked away," slightly under the influence of a few glasses of wine, with this man holding me by the hand as we went in search of a location on-site where we could sit and talk. He insisted on getting to know me, and although I felt a strong urge to resist, there was an unnatural pull towards him, which I yielded to. We chatted. I had more wine; he had a beer. He spoke about his upbringing in several parts of the world, his African heritage, and the challenges of being bullied while living there. He shared about studying in London, being in the army, and being headhunted by some of the world's renowned organisations—all before the age of thirty. I was so taken with him that I could not remember anything remotely remarkable about myself to share. Thank God for the tension-breaker with a joke we shared about how quickly, after we finished our drink, the waiter brought our bill and how it might have been because we were black. It was a bad joke, but we found it terribly amusing. In the midst of entertaining ourselves, he happened to mention that he was engaged to be married. I knew that was my cue to escape from the intoxicating hold of this man. I sought to flee to my hotel, which was thankfully right across the road from the event we were at, while I tried to come off as unaffected by his cavalier admission. This man, seeing right through my attempts and using his charm, grasped an opportunity to kiss me, to which I responded by initially pulling away and then surrendering as he held my face ever so intentionally. It was surreal how much the thoughts in my head were fully opposed to my bodily actions. It was inexplicable. While being held in his arms, I found myself uttering the words, "This is so wrong," and suddenly, the dream came back to mind. *My gosh!* It took me long enough to finally remember "the warning" I received before I came on the trip! Once I remembered, I sobered up fast and scurried to my hotel, and that was the last time I ever saw or spoke to Mr. British.

God has always met me in the most interesting spaces and precarious situations. It has been a longstanding characteristic of our relationship. When no one else is there for me to ventilate the curious musings of my heart, He has always made Himself present and almost tangible in those moments. I have never felt closer to God than in some of my lowest places. Unfiltered emotions and all, God gives me the freedom and space to pour out my deepest aches, and more often than not, I feel lighter, even when the circumstances have not changed. In addition, God seems to always position the right person or people in my midst to help walk me through my darkest times.

That night I returned to my hotel room and was greeted by my colleague who I was sharing the room with, who I had effectively ditched to have a drink with Mr. British. She was so gracious and so excited about my "romantic rendezvous." Little did she know, at the time, how much regret was creeping upon me and would soon consume me. When she retired to bed, I went to the bathroom and called my best friend back in Jamaica, who, although there was a 13-hour time difference, still managed to make herself available as she always does. I told her about how I met someone and the thrill of all the events leading up to the unfortunate and incredibly anti-climactic ending. She experienced every emotion with me, and I automatically felt less alone. Less foolish. Eventually, I was able to get some sleep that night, despite trying to figure out how to respond to his unwelcome text regarding our time together: "That was brilliant."

Another interesting experience I recall was the time I had been spared a very abusive relationship. I was in Raleigh, North Carolina, when a kind woman, young at heart and lively with the best storytelling skills and a Southern accent, picked me up and took me to a fancy coffee shop. After meeting for the first time and chatting casually as if we were old friends, she became pensive, and soon, she told me that she felt a pull to share something dark and personal. She shared about how she was happily married before it painfully descended into a life-threatening situation from which God helped her to escape. Her husband, who previously partnered with her in counselling youth at their church, had become an abuser who she could no longer recognise, and before she knew it, she was trying to strategize how to save her life. He went from being her life companion and faithful youth group co-leader to becoming her worst nightmare—talk about a transformation. But the question was, why in the world was I hearing this story? Why would God impress it on her heart to share this with me; someone she was meeting for the first time with no prior knowledge of my relationship history?

It so happened that not long before that time in Raleigh, I had met a man I was oddly attracted to. I say "oddly" because I went from totally overlooking him to suddenly being ensnared by his charm. When I consider this event in my life, it is important for me to bear in mind the circumstances of my life at that time. I was twenty-five, the youngest person on the management team of a multinational company in Kingston. I reported to the country manager, who often turned to intimidation to drive productivity. It was not exactly a fun position to be in, even if it did help me to grow exponentially. At that time, I was hungry for support. Any support.

When I met this man, I remember just how completely unaware I was despite his public profile, and I felt a bit embarrassed when he eventually introduced himself. As I got to know him, betraying the part of me that had a bad feeling about things based on bits of information I learned about him and signs I had seen, I began to view our meeting as some sort of blessing in disguise. In my mind, he would be the perfect person to help me secure some business relationships with the respective stakeholders—a daunting task that was one of my job requirements—and I could not see it being possible any other way except through him. The only problem is that while a lot of good was developing from this budding relationship, a lot worse was in store that would outweigh the good.

The first time I welcomed him to my home represented a breach of my personal space in a way that I was totally unprepared for. I was coming out of a painful break-up, which all but helped me feel vulnerable and misguided in my interactions with this person. More than anything, I wanted to explore the development of a professional relationship, but it was clear that he found me attractive, and, honestly, the attention from him was alluring. The inevitable occurred: we began to date, which only made room for confusion and unmet expectations for both of us. I had no business entering into that kind of relationship, coming fresh out of a break-up and wanting to maintain professional boundaries, and to make matters worse, I knew we did not share the same values and Christian convictions. I had chosen foolishly to compromise those convictions and my relationship with God.

As the time progressed, our communication worsened. He became less available at his convenience, and I wrestled internally with having shared so much of myself with someone I had not first established a solid foundation with. I had one of those moments when the girl felt conflicted with herself because of the choices she had made, and out of frustration, she began to make demands. In my case, I wanted him to clarify "what we were." Did he have intentions of building a future with me? I was doubtful of a future with him, in truth, but I was already in this situation and felt that his answer would help me somehow manage my emotions. When he did not give an answer, it was as if I had turned off a switch to cope, and I became nonchalant and cold towards him. Things came to a crashing end when I went out with someone else and told him, with every intention to prove a point. Well, he responded by turning on a switch. He transformed into the person I had heard rumours about: a verbally abusive and manipulative beast who I seemed to have awakened. His anger was palpable, and when he said, "You have no idea who you are dealing with," I took it as a strong warning, but even then, I wished we could turn back the hands of time and try again. What a strange desire to have when one sees the danger ahead. Thankfully, God intervened and caused the door of communication to be tightly shut between us. It was the solution I needed to come back to my senses and to realise how crazy it was for me to have been actually desiring another chance at a relationship with this man.

This experience was unfortunate and completely avoidable. As I reflected on that day we met, I realized how the trajectory of things could have taken a different path had I made healthier choices and upheld the necessary boundaries. I sensed the danger approaching from our conversations, our interactions, and my choosing to compromise my beliefs, yet I continued to be a participant, leading to my demise. In spite of this truth, God's grace was beyond evident. He had spared me from much worse that lay ahead if I had continued on that path, and I realised that the experience gave me a brief window into the internal struggle many women in abusive relationships face: the struggle of deciding whether to give up or stay. Should I leave this person who is not all bad, someone I have developed feelings for, who has shown care towards me? If only we could go back and pretend this fall-out never happened. Or should I take this as a sign of worse to come and leave while I am still able? "Tek sleep mark death," as the Jamaican proverb goes.

Well, I have no doubt that many women have found themself in a similar position, contemplating these same variables. Thank God He made the decision for me and allowed the door to be locked through the man's insistence on blocking me from his life. To think I was feeling like the "victim" and yet I was the one being blocked, but the truth is, we were both hurting individuals and dealing with things in different but equally unhealthy ways.

God allows messy situations to unfold at times so we can more easily see how desperately we need His intervention. I recall ordering a particular book on Amazon by C.S. Lewis as a gift that I believed would enhance his spiritual life; it was slightly presumptuous and ridiculous of me when I look back at it now. Well, when things came to an end, I checked my Amazon account randomly and saw that the order had been mysteriously canceled. To this day, I cannot explain how this happened, but needless to say, God was making it very clear that the chapter with this person was closed. What was also clear was that God is more deeply vested in our lives than we realise. I guarantee this, not just for me but for all of us. He pays attention to the details—the big and the small—and there are times when He intervenes in overt or covert ways. Even when God appears not to intervene, there is a message for us, but we must pray for the ability to discern what He is doing and saying in each unique situation. He is always actively at work in our lives.

A HAPPY GIRL'S SADNESS

A once content girl
Who has lost her happiness
Is like a vigorous sea
Void of its waves;
A rose shed of its petals;
A smile-less face.
She's stifled by gloom
Her tears overflowed for days.
Never has a heart felt as heavy
As that of a sad girl
Who was once happy.

She paces aimlessly
As she questions herself.
Her mind is a maze,
Not even she knows the way out.
For the depth of her sorrow
Flows deeper than a stream
It overcomes hurdles of constant glee
And manifests into a state of emptiness,
A condition called sadness.
A venomous stronghold that sucks her dry.

Nothing is like a happy girl
Who becomes so sad that she could die.
Like a dark grey cloud

Looming across a brilliant blue sky.
The earth shakes with every painful sigh.
She cries, sobs, weeps and bawls
For the pain she must endure
Feels like more than she can haul.

But at last! At the end of the dark, lonely tunnel
Is a light.
A light for which she must fight.
For at the end of the mourning
Comes the day that God has made
She will look to the skies
And her strength she will regain.
And that will be the end of the sadness
From the content girl who lost her happiness
... almost.

HATE IS THE WORST DISEASE

You, miss lady
Yes, you.
I am not moved by your intimidating stare
Your dismissive demeanour
Daring, dark, cold shoulder.

Cynical remarks
Through your devious half-grin
No. I am not afraid
Of your illicit judgment
Trying to cast me in the box
That is your narrow mind
The eyes that see me as
"Less than" or "unworthy"
Do not sway me one bit.
For I am firmly rooted
And you, my dear,
Have barked up the wrong tree.
I will not receive your hurtful words
Dripping in disdain and deceit
Wafting a faint scent of jealousy
Oh, mistake not my meekness for weakness
My silence does not reflect defeat
For at the appointed time, I will strike
My words will be like arrows
Straight and to the point

Piercing like darts or like a bee's sting
The impact akin to it's venom

I am a beautiful princess-warrior
My battles you cannot see
And those I've fought and those to come
I've already won victoriously.
You may choose to hate me
Seethe with rage when you see my face
Cringe when you hear my name
Meanwhile, for your healing, I will pray.
Hate is the worst disease
It promises a life of bitterness and misery
The eternal answer is love
And thankfully, I am surrounded by love
Surviving on love
Loved by Love
Empowered to love you.

AGAIN

Last night, I cried again
Which makes me realise
Every time I feel strong
I am reminded I am weak.

I keep thinking I am over it
I keep feeling like I have bounced back
Only to realise that healing needs more than time
Healing seems to be never-ending.

Still, memories remain fresh
Still, my love persists
Still, the hurts, hurt
Still, I cry.

Last night, I cried again
And couldn't help but wonder why
As the tears trickled down my face
Soon I can't breathe, as the lumps form in my throat.

These are the times I remember
I can fall so far into despair
It's hard to pull myself out
My strength fails me... again.

Last night I cried again
I stared in the mirror at myself
'Til my face was stained and stiff
I fell asleep that night with a frozen face.

Today is a new day; I feel strong
But I know the tears are near
For it was only last night that I cried
And perhaps I will cry again today and tomorrow.

WHOLE-HEARTED LOVE

Love the Lord with all your heart
Said a wise woman of old
But how can I love wholly, I asked,
With a heart that isn't whole?

She smiled and looked up
As if reminiscing on times passed
Every little broken heart, she said,
Will surely mend at last.

Be grateful for every day.
Start by just being you
You can read and cry and play
Do all the things you love to do.

Slowly but surely
My dear, you will heal
And even as you grieve at times
Little secrets will the Lord reveal.

Eventually, you will find
As you spend more time with Him
That weight of brokenness you once felt
Begins to finally subside.

Soon, my love, your heart will be whole

And you will be ready to fly!
To soar on wings of strength and courage
To love faster than the twinkling of an eye.

PERSONAL REFLECTIONS

1. Describe a time in your life when you felt so brokenhearted you never thought you would recover.

2. What was it that helped you get closer to feeling like yourself during that time of deep sadness?

3. Who were the people in your life that God sent to comfort you at that time? Recall them by name, write them down if you desire, and take a moment to be thankful.

4. Would you describe yourself as someone who willingly shares your struggles, or are you likely to keep them to yourself? Explain why you describe yourself as such.

5. Take a moment to remember that time of sadness and put in words what you want to say to God about that situation. The words of Psalm 141 may be used as a guide.

Chapter 5

Singleness, My SuperPower

"Anyone who believes in me will do the same works I have done, and even greater works, because I am going to be with the Father." (John 14:12 - NLT).

"If you could choose a superpower, what would it be?" is a question that is regularly used as an icebreaker in team meetings. It is an interesting way to learn more about people and how their minds work. The ability to be invisible, to know people's thoughts, or to travel in time could be seen as abilities that defy reality as we know it. With the superpower comes a problem-solving component, as there is no need for power unless there is a challenge. Maybe being invisible, for example, could help you with the personal challenge of disliking human interaction if you are an introvert. To know people's thoughts; actually, it is hard to imagine what problems one could solve with this power; it seems more like it would have an opposite effect and instead invite problems. The bottom line is that for every problem we face, we all desire a special ability to overcome them so we do not have to deal with whatever the impact of the problems are that awaits us.

When asked to give a perspective on superpowers and why they fascinate us, ChatGPT had this to say:

> *"Superpowers are often described as extraordinary abilities that go beyond human capabilities, symbolising what we might wish we could do in times of crisis or when faced with challenges. They represent our deepest desires for control, justice, and the ability to overcome our limitations. As a cultural phenomena, superpowers tap into our collective imagination, allowing us to explore themes of morality, identity, and the human condition in a fantastical context."*

ChatGPT goes on to reference the book *Super Heroes: A Modern Mythology* by Richard Reynolds, where the concept of superheroes and superpowers are explored widely, looking into how they have changed over time and why they are so important in modern culture. It examines the association of superheroes as emblems of strength, justice, and our innate desire to penetrate all human barriers.[1]

Suppose you took a moment to consider some of the deepest, personal barriers we face as people, like fear, rejection,

---

[1] Reynolds, Richard. Super Heroes: A Modern Mythology. University Press of Mississippi, 1992.

loneliness, heartbreak, etc. What would superpowers look like to overcome such challenges? I believe that a person who really knows they are loved, regardless of their relationship status, regardless of how people treat them; one who lives and loves freely while feeling completely secure in themselves is a person who is undefeatable. That, for me, is the goal, and I have seen how my life as a single person was a solid training ground for me to get there. The goal may seem unattainable, and maybe, in reality, it is reserved for the only One I know who achieved this during His life as a man on earth. Nevertheless, I hold on to the promise Jesus left us before He ascended into heaven: *"Anyone who believes in me will do the same works I have done, and even greater works, because I am going to be with the Father."* (John 14:12 - NLT). Let us think back on some of these works that Jesus did: resurrecting a man who was dead in a tomb for four days (see John 11:17), walking on water (see Matthew 14:25), and commanding a storm to seize (see Mark 4:39). Jesus proves that unlike the fantastical powers conjured up by mere man's imagination, this kind of power comes from the living God Himself and is more real than life itself. Furthermore, having Jesus as an Advocate makes all the difference, as highlighted in the last few words of the verse: *"because I am going to be with the Father." (see John 14:12 - NLT)*. The next verse expounds on how Jesus being in heaven works in our favour, and it clearly instructs us how to obtain this ultimate power from Him: *"You can ask for anything in my name, and I will do it, so that the Son can bring glory to the Father." (John 14:13 - NLT)*.

While meditating on these scriptures, it struck me that there is a correlation between having superpowers and being dependent on Christ, and what better time to learn dependence on Him than during singleness.

When I was intentional about being single, I had the best opportunity to focus on how I was wired, why I made the choices I made, what my wounds were—both the healed and unhealed—and what were my deepest fears, among many more concerns. In the same way a soldier must prepare for battle by understanding their opponent's weaknesses and, even more so, their own, so too must we treat the spiritual war for our hearts. We must acknowledge and recognize the nature of our enemy and his tactics, and we must study and guard ourselves accordingly.

In this context, true singleness has to do with choosing to prioritise your personal, spiritual, and even professional growth over romantic pursuits. In true singleness, you are focused on you but not in an obnoxious, self-absorbed way where nothing and no one else matters, lest you run the risk of becoming narcissistic. It is a time to recover from past hurts and rediscover things that bring you joy outside of a romantic relationship where you have to consider a partner's needs. It is also a time to perhaps serve people in different capacities that are wholesome and fulfilling.

I remember only at the end of a three-year relationship with someone who had loved a particular type of music was when

I realised that I did not really enjoy that type of music. All along, while we were together, I would tolerate it since he had liked it so much, but when we broke up, and I was regaining a sense of my likes and dislikes, I came to uncover my own taste in music. It reminds me of a scene in the romantic comedy "Runaway Bride" where Julia Roberts' favourite eggs always changed based on whoever she was in a relationship with at the time. When she was finally unattached to anyone, she was able to discover what her favourite type of eggs were: eggs benedict.

Singleness can present an opportunity to be awakened to your true identity, and conversely, when we do not know ourselves well enough, we can lose the sense of our own self when we are tied up in relationships that demand much from us: our time, energy, affections, and thoughts. According to the Bible, all of these are precious and worth protecting at all costs. Proverbs 4:23 says, *"Guard your heart above all else, for it determines the course of your life." (NLT)*. Some interpretations say, *"Keep your heart."* This perfectly captures the posture that true singleness bears: a picture of someone gently holding their heart, nurturing it, feeding it, and handing it over as the Father instructs.

At a point in my journey, this looked like declining what might have appeared to be a simple lunch or dinner invitation out of an abundance of caution. This did not mean I was a hermit with no social life, as my dependence on community and group settings greatly increased (more on that in the next chapter). Rather, I chose to keep at minimum intimate one-on-one interactions with persons of the opposite sex, especially with the ones I felt more attracted to. This was not easy by any means, and did require a level of self-deprivation, which is a completely foreign concept in this society that is all about self-indulgence.

I recall a situation when someone I came to know, who I saw only as a friend but who had stronger feelings for me, would extend kindness in multiple ways. I was offered everything from dinners to monetary assistance, transportation, and help with random tasks, and he lived only minutes from my house. Sometimes "falling" into a romantic relationship is the easiest and most attractive option, especially when we meet people who seem to fulfil our most natural longings; but if singleness is the catalyst for our superpowers to take full effect, then entering a relationship out of convenience is kryptonite.

SWEET FEELING

I've tasted many a sweet feeling
Romantic dining, the finest of wines
Climbed climaxes at the highest of heights
Fought hard in the name of love
Strived tirelessly for love
Ate of sweet fruits, turned bitter
Dribbled the ball that was in my court
As I played with romance
Until it threw (me) in the towel
Precious time passed as we waltzed 'til sundown.

But down on me did the Son set His eyes
Never to leave His sight
His face fixed like a flint
As at Calvary
While this treasured gem He so perspired after
Found herself in just about the hands
Of any charming suitor that crossed.
Still, His pursuit was relentless
Even when waves of deceit and lust
Washed up close enough to her heart.

The taste of sweet feeling I have not lacked
Drunk on fantasy and wondrous earthly things
Feasted on fruits of labour
Frolicked in the splendour of the moonlight

Lost in the eclipses of carnal pleasures unspoken
Caught in the snare of an empty, soul-less,
unfulfilling abyss called temporary gratification
That is sometimes deathly permanent.
Yet, my new love sweetens more than my tongue
It satisfies my soul.

We take long walks and walk hand in hand
The Author of Love Himself and I
I lay my deepest, darkest secrets at His feet
Where they are safe.
I am safe; He saved me.
Now I drink His living water
It quenches my thirst like I've never known
He whispers secrets of times gone and to come
There is nothing ugly about this love
No perverse thrill gained from envy and jealousy.

No sweeter feeling than this have I known
The feeling of assurance.

Blessed assurance
A love that cannot be denied or questioned
Even the 'sweetest taboo' comes second
A love so good cannot be contained
There is a world that awaits its sweet taste,
Desperate without even knowing it
I will tell them: Many a sweet feeling I've tasted
But only one has called me His, and I call Him mine.

PRINCE OF PEACE, PRINCE OF POWER

Prince of Peace
You ravaged through storms
Of restless, broken relationships
Bursting through layers of pain
Hardened by time and expectations unmet
You gently lowered my walls.

Erected by fear
You chased me relentlessly
Even as I ran far from You
Even as I was swayed by the winds
Tempted by lies
You barged in to my rescue
Never letting up on your commitment
You are so faithful.

You have fought hard for me
To the point of death.
Oh, what a love like yours!
You open the eyes of my heart
And yet
I will never understand.
I will never understand.

PERSONAL REFLECTIONS

1. Was there a time in your life when you felt loved and adored? Express it here. (If you cannot recall such a time, write about your desire in this regard).

2. Has anyone ever shown you an extraordinary act of love when you felt you were least deserving of it? How did that make you feel? If you have never experienced that, how do you imagine you would feel?

3. What do you think it means to have an encounter with the love of Jesus?

4. What are some of the primary ways you enjoy expressing yourself to those you love? Do you use words, show them by giving them a gift or by being physically affectionate? Do you show your love by spending quality time with the person or by serving them in a way they appreciate?

5. Describe the perfect day you would enjoy with Jesus. How would you choose to spend time if it was just you and Him?

Chapter 6

Born to Belong (God Made Us For Community)

"Do not fear, for I have redeemed you; I have called you by name; you are mine." (Isaiah 43:1b - NIV).

Who do you belong to? We have been designed in the image and likeness of God, the Father, the Son, and the Holy Spirit, who exist individually and collectively in community. They are interdependent; one does not exist without the other; they belong to each other. There is also a divine order where the Son does not operate outside of the Father, and the Spirit does not operate outside of the Son. We too have been created to function similarly in terms of communing with God and fellow man in a particular divine order: with God, we are to function in full dependence on Him, and with fellow humans created to function independently and interdependently. This concept has been a pillar in my life that has kept me in God's fold pretty much my entire life. Even before I was aware enough to acknowledge it, this fact remained true despite my wavering levels of commitment at different intervals.

I grew up attending a relatively small local church, planted in partnership by a group of young, zealous Christians, including my mother, along with an overseas church that shared the same understanding and convictions surrounding doctrine from the Bible. I was privileged to build a fairly close relationship with aunties and uncles, some of whom were childhood friends of my mother, while making lifelong associations with a handful of people in my age group. I experienced a type of intimacy at church that many do not get to partake of as visitors or members of big churches. Unfortunately, outside of the days that we assembled, I did not connect much with my church family, so after a while, the roots planted in my childhood struggled to expand. Still, the exposure to Christ and the Christian community that I was afforded by the church I was raised in has been a cornerstone of my spiritual development.

God was faithful in seeing my need and deep longing for connection to a wider net of people I could identify with, who were serving Him joyfully; a void I believe was an inevitable result of being part of a "micro church" locally. I found myself searching for such people, and God helped me to find them. In fact, He gave me more than I had asked for and brought community to my doorstep—or Facebook message inbox, if we are being literal.

I previously mentioned the group of women I was warmly welcomed into on account of my high school mate (who messaged me on Facebook). That served as a starting point for me to recognise the importance of regular fellowship with believers outside of the typical church setting. In this intimate space, I could share many more details about my day-to-day life: challenges at work, bosses, and coworkers, struggles at home, and following all that sharing, we prayed.

Another imperative benefit of these smaller group settings was that I developed a love for the Word of God. Finally, the scriptures came to life in a way that was personal, and gradually, my relationship with Christ grew deeper. As my understanding of God increased, so did my awareness of what was wrong and right; things I had not considered before now became matters of contemplation. For instance, I remember my first Bible Study facilitator lovingly sharing about her son, who exhibited a passion for the Lord at a young age and who boldly proclaimed Jesus to his peers. We essentially fell within the same age group, and I recall being at a gathering among friends where he was a speaker. A question posed that night by a believer, like most of us, was, *"I am in a relationship with someone who is not a Christian. What should I do?"* The young man's unashamed and unpopular response was a resolute, *"You have to come out of that relationship."* Most of us there nodded out of respect for his position, but deep down, I know most of us felt the same inwardly, that his response was exactly what we did not want to hear. So often, we find ourselves in that position, confronted by the unequivocal counter-cultural truth of God.

The easy way to respond is to just nod, not necessarily because we have been convicted and are repentant, but just out of respect for the person's stance. Almost like, *"That is great for you to be at that place. I love that for you,"* but somehow we dismiss ourselves from the message being necessary for our own lives as well. This tendency to separate ourselves when God has sent out a message intended for all of us hinders our own growth and transformation that we truly need. We end up being guilty of being hearers and not doers of His Word, which the Bible condemns as it is a sure path to deceiving oneself.

My exposure to more peers living boldly for Christ and honouring the Word of God in spite of imperfections began to increase, and eventually, I was thriving among a fairly wide net of believers. We came from different backgrounds; some of us went to the same high schools, lived within close enough proximity, and, most of all, shared a special connection through the Holy Spirit. We were far from perfect, but we sought after the Lord, and eventually, these Tuesday evening gatherings easily became the highlight of my week. I was so impacted by this environment that I became known for regularly inviting people from all walks of life to attend. After all, we were meeting in fairly comfortable homes, learning the Word of God, sharing our life journeys, and praying for each other, all while engaging in fun activities—what was not to love. I genuinely felt like my life was enriched, and I felt deeply grateful for this.

To this day, I can still rejoice at the role of community based on how it has unfolded personally. Naturally, there have been negative factors to deal with, including occasional 'fall-outs,' persons choosing to no longer walk closely with Christ, disappointments, discouragement, changing dynamics of people coming and going for different reasons, and the vast impact of the pandemic, among other challenges. Nevertheless, what I have gained far surpasses what I have lost, if I have lost anything.

Dealing with difficult aspects of relationships with people is part and parcel of the Christian journey. If we always agreed, how would our flawed thoughts and behaviours be challenged? How can there be accountability without certain things being confronted? I am indebted to my brothers and sisters in Christ who saw me operating in a manner that was not reflective of the work of Jesus in my heart, and I have experienced being corrected in gentleness, truth, and grace. Of course, there are instances when I have either received or issued correction harshly, and at times, it was mistakenly all hard truth and no grace or too much grace and not enough truth. Either way, I see the importance of community being underscored here—that we need these spaces to learn and practice how to actively obey God and show the love of Christ no matter our age or stage of maturity, as quite frankly, it will not come naturally for most of us.

We are all dealing with flawed upbringings in one way or another, personality traits, poor past experiences that have scarred and limped us in some way, attitudes and behaviours that do not always align with the character and nature of Christ, but we are a work in progress, and that is worth celebrating. The best learning ground before we can reach out to the rest of the world is in the unity of those who also identify as soldiers of Christ.

I recall when I was approached to be part of a video, playing the role of a female politician, a former Ms. World. She had come under heavy scrutiny for posting a picture of herself in a swimsuit on social media by a renowned religious figure known for his work in addressing poverty in Jamaica. The video was a satirical response to the concept and theme song written by a popular comedian known for highlighting social injustice and for being a deist (believing in a Supreme Being but in no way religious). We connected on many levels. We shared views about women unjustly being scrutinised, such as in the case of the politician, and I really felt impassioned about defending her. After all, why should this woman be publicly criticised for wearing a swimsuit to the beach? And why should she not have the right to post a picture of herself in said swimsuit (with a t-shirt on, mind you) even as a public figure, and one who years ago earned a title on behalf of her country that claimed her to be the most beautiful woman in the world? Incidentally, that title she earned for her country required her to wear a swimsuit for a global audience, yet here she is now being harshly criticised for the same thing. I was prepared to stand up for justice, so I agreed to be part of the video despite its irreverence and suggestiveness. I failed to consider that my doing the video would paint me as staunchly against the religious figure when I had respected him greatly.

120

I regarded him as a brother in Christ and admired his impact on our country. However, I disagreed with his position and actions in this instance. I suddenly realised that maybe being part of the video was not the way I wanted to respond to the situation, but by then, I had already shot day 1 of 2 days of the video shoot. When I made the audacious request to no longer be part of the video, it was completely disregarded, and understandably so: production costs were high, and time and energy had already been invested. There was no turning back for the comedian, who was very excited about his project, even if it meant hiring a doppelgänger to fill my role for the parts I had opted out of shooting. It was a disaster that had only just begun.

The video was released and quickly went viral, raking in thousands of views; I wished I could disappear. I watched it, and yes, I chuckled at parts as it was inherently funny, but the snide comments from viewers would quickly sober me. I remember sitting in a meeting with one of the clients at the ad agency I worked at during that time when he made an inappropriate comment about my body after having seen the video. When he saw my facial reaction, he justified his comment by saying, "*Well, you put yourself out there, so you must expect this kind of thing.*" I suppose I did "*put myself out there*" and thereby opened a door granting people of poor character and no tact unsolicited access to pass unacceptable remarks, especially in professional settings.

For a while, the video was a topic of conversation in many of my social and other groups, and it had become the centre of attention among a Jamaican Facebook group for atheists. I remember watching myself prancing in the video that was being used as a tool of ridicule, not just towards the religious figure but also to the Christian community at large. My image was being used to mock the God I served and the community I was part of that had played such a key role in my life, and I could do nothing about it but watch and wait for the hype to end while praying for forgiveness and mercy.

Fellow Christians were offended and hurt, and people were disappointed—not exactly the outcome I was going for when I went ahead with the project. I felt like I had allowed Satan this chance to make a fool of me and my values in this public way, but I knew it was going to be a powerful learning lesson for the future.

This experience gave me the opportunity to experience the real value of a loving Christian community. Yes, there were those Christians who judged me harshly and wrongfully dealt with me out of offence like they had never made mistakes before. But there were vastly more of those who stood by my side, had conversations with me to understand my thought process leading up to the decision to do the video, gave me advice on how to handle the situation, and showed me love during a time of great self-condemnation. As a show of reconciliation, and for my peace of mind, my brother in Christ, G, and his wife supported me as I wrote letters to both the religious figure and the politician, apologising for my part in the video. To the politician, I expressed my position and let her know that I did not believe the video was the best way to represent her or myself. I knew that it might have been a bit strange for her to have received an apology, given the video was made in her favour and defence, but my conviction was immovable at this point—this video was not the most honourable way to represent any of the parties involved and, hence, not the Christ-like thing to do, no matter how comedic/entertaining it was.

It is interesting to witness God's redeemable ways unfold amidst the broken world we live in, where people are imperfect. After receiving my letter, the religious man who had headed an international Jesuit ministry based in Jamaica wanted to meet me. He invited me for a full tour of the work of his organisation in repressed parts of Kingston, where they serve the most destitute of people, those unwanted and discarded by their families due to mental and physical disabilities, and we visited a home for girls who were teenage mothers. I had not been aware of the extent of the work prior to this visit, so the opportunity to do the tour of all the facilities is something I appreciated greatly, and I saw it as God's way of reaffirming *"all things work together for good for those who love God and are called according to His purpose."* I really did not have anything to worry about, even if I had made a mistake that would live on the internet 'forever,' and although I had faced the consequences, God never left me alone to deal with it.

NOTHING MATTERS

Surrounded by happiness
But unable to feel it
Every moment of glee
Is short-lived
After the excitement quiets
And I'm left alone with my thoughts
The silence is piercing
And I wish I could escape
Reaching out to others is calming
For a moment
But when they leave
Despair consumes again
But it's then
I can hear the small voice
In the stillness
In the eye of the agony
When continuing to live
Seems unbearable
If life should continue like this
Too painful to even imagine
The voice still prevails
His word resounds
Through music,
His Word dances to melodies in my thoughts
The reality of human brokenness

Our predisposed condition
Born under a sentence of death
When you're faced with how real life is
It is overwhelming
We are all so messed up
Tainted
Flawed
Desperately wicked, yet not without hope
For those who ever come to know
The hope that exists
But, Lord, why this way?
Why such a painful existence?
This mystery
I will never understand
I am in pieces.

PERSONAL REFLECTIONS

1. Disappointment can hit hard in relationships, especially when the expectations we have of a person, especially those we depend on, are unmet. What do you notice about yourself when you feel disappointed by someone close to you? Make a note of any recurring actions or thought patterns you exhibit (for example, the thought, "This is why I will never trust anyone").

2. Do you actively try to avoid being hurt or disappointed by others? What methods do you usually employ to do this?

3. Are you considered closed off or having a wall up by those closest to you, and would you be regarded as one who takes correction well?

4. Whatever your answers to the above, take a moment to pray and ask the Holy Spirit to tell you why you are the way you are. Write what you are sensing.

5. Thank God in prayer for the information you just received, repent of the ways that have not been like Christ, and forgive those who have hurt you, calling them by name. Ask God now to help you find a

healthy community that will make you feel safe in being vulnerable and building solid Christian relationships. Write anything additional you are sensing from God.

Chapter 7

Obedience Over Sacrifice

"To obey is better than sacrifice, and to heed is better than the fat of rams." (1 Samuel 15:22b - NIV).

"*I* cannot be in a relationship with someone who is not a Christian,***"** I remember saying aloud as I reflected and thought about what my life experiences had taught me. Relationships of the past saw me making allowances out of being "reasonable" and "understanding" of people's different convictions while compromising my beliefs. I gave men the benefit of the doubt, even when they had made it very clear that they did not share my faith, views on God, or values and were not interested in doing so. It took yet another low point for me to recognise that if I continued to disobey God by choosing to entertain men like these, many of whom had wonderful qualities, I would be facing an existence of no peace, constant anxiety, and worry about the future bound by fear of failure in relationships. This is no way for one to live, and it was certainly not the way God intended for me to live.

The decision to yield to obedience to God, that is, doing relationships according to Biblical teaching, has been challenging, but it has also been completely freeing. By now, I have realised that life works out much more favourably when I listen to God rather than resist Him. When you wear the seal of Christ, the reality is that no matter what decisions you make, God, in His lovingkindness, ensures that your life aligns with exactly what He had planned from the beginning of time, but do not be mistaken, the resistance we put up in the interim can have a devastating impact that often is more than we bargained for.

Imagine that before the beginning of time, God already destined your path, and yet that path somehow manages to merge with the decisions we make of our own free will, which was also given to us by God. When I think about an example of this, I consider how when I was younger, I had aspirations of being a singer, but when people encouraged me to become a gospel singer specifically, the thought was less than appealing to me. As I got older, pursuing the craft and eventually growing in my faith, I naturally tended towards singing gospel/faith-related songs. Without much thought, singing music that glorifies God has become more and more a part of my everyday life, and it makes me smile knowing that despite me dismissing the thought in the past, God had already destined that this is where I would end up eventually.

There is a correlation between obedience and trauma, I have realised. For instance, there were many times I recall when I was younger, as far back as my early teens, I dreaded being in certain situations with the opposite sex. These scenarios could vary from walking past a group of older men, being alone in a space, like a workplace, with a man who you genuinely want to have a professional relationship with but who clearly has ill motives and the sickening feeling that would come over me the moment I noticed either a look or heard something in their voice. Most females have been conditioned to pick up on certain cues easily, depending on the social and cultural contexts. For instances like those, some of which were at times traumatising, obedience likely had very little to do with the situation.

That being said, quite often, the trouble we find ourselves in is directly tied to an act of rebellion or defiance, a stubbornness that is hell-bent on doing what one wills while totally disregarding every piece of good advice you have ever received. Selena Gomez put it perfectly in her song *"The Heart Wants What It Wants."* Unfortunately, what the heart wants frequently is not what it needs. When we consider the heart in these terms, and in the terms it is referenced in the Bible, I believe it is referring to that place where our emotions are stored and processed. When we have gone through negative experiences, that place is inevitably influenced directly, and depending on the tools we have to manage our emotions, it can become a storing place for a lot of filth. The heart is said to be "desperately wicked," according to Jeremiah 7. When I think deeply about those two descriptive words, "desperate" and "wicked," I think of something terrible that is hopeless or incapable of producing good without divine intervention. I wholeheartedly believe this is true.

Let's take, for example, the painful experience I had of the breakup with my Christian boyfriend and the resentment and anger that had developed even before the hurtful breakup. They were stored up in a place inside of me (my heart), and the impact of that experience was greater because of the deeper pain of an estranged emotional relationship with my father which, at this point, was never processed nor addressed. This then led to my operating in a wounded, hurt, insecure manner that was now compounded by anger and resentment specifically exacted towards Christian men because of this failed romantic relationship. What then became my driving force was rebellion and a conscious decision to defy what I had known to be against God's will and commandment: *"Do not be unequally yoked with unbelievers." (2 Corinthians 6:14 - ESV)* in relationships. I knew this, not only because it is written in scripture but from the standpoint of already paying the painful price with previous love interests who did not share my beliefs. However, the door had been opened as a result of the new heartbreak, and even if I did not "actively" pursue being in such relationships, my passive participation by simply entertaining non-Christian suitors ended up being just as detrimental. Satan saw his chance to kick me while I was down, knowing my defenses and my faith were weak, and I consequently made decisions that did nothing except cause more devastation and heartbreak. So goes the cycle of heartbreak, disobedience, and trauma.

The silver lining is that obedience can be learned, and yes, most times it is learned the hard way, that is, after we have made the error and faced a consequence, but we can take comfort in the fact that Jesus himself had to "learn obedience" according to Hebrews 5:8 which says, *"Though he were a Son, yet learned he obedience by the things which he suffered;" (KJV).* This puts a lot into perspective. Firstly, imagine God's only begotten Son, who was the epitome of perfection; though He was without blemish and completely blameless, He still had the need to "learn obedience" from the things He suffered while living in His human state on earth. If He had to learn it, how much more would we, as imperfect beings, born into this world? This struggle is not something that takes God by surprise; yet, failure to abide by His Word can leave us grappling with unfathomable and devastating effects. At the same time, many seem to get away with murder when we observe their defiance towards God. They are unapologetic, some are oblivious, and others are outrightly rebellious and dismissive of God's Word with intent, and they seem to never suffer any consequences, living their best lives. But the Bible iterates that *"He causes his sun to rise on the evil and the good, and sends rain on the righteous and the unrighteous." (Matthew 5:45 - NIV).* God holds within His hands the power to allow persons to face harsh consequences, but His mercy is often extended, and we tend to take that for granted. There is no act we can commit that God is not already aware of before, and He is also aware of what the effects of those actions will be, whether now or later, whether this generation or the next.

PERSONAL REFLECTIONS

1. What are your thoughts on the concept of Jesus, the Son of God, 'learning obedience'?

2. On a scale of 1 - 10, 10 being the highest, how would you rate your ability to learn obedience?

3. What are the hindrances to your obedience to God? Write them down, and bring the list before the Lord in your next prayer time.

4. Recall a time you disobeyed God's Word. What was that experience like, and what was the outcome?

5. If you can, identify how the Lord extended grace in this same example.

6. Say a prayer of forgiveness for disobeying God and ask for His help to navigate the path He has in store for you.

Chapter 8

Faithfulness Yields Fruit

"But the fruit of the Spirit is love, joy, peace, patience, kindness, goodness, faithfulness, gentleness, self-control; against such things there is no law." (Galatians 5:22-23 - ESV).

God holds the keys to our future. I might have always believed this to be true in theory, but it was not until I got closer to being married that the truth of that statement started to hit home.

I met my husband one day while helping a close friend and mentor. Her car was out of commission, and she needed a ride to the supermarket. As fate would have it, just as we pulled out of her driveway and began our journey, he turned onto the road enroute to his house across from hers. They were neighbours, and he would have been her first choice for the supermarket stop had he been available. As it turns out, he freed up just in time for us to be introduced in the middle of the road between our respective car windows. You could say it was romantic, except I did not think too much of the introduction at the time. I mean, I found him easy on the eyes, but for me, the thoughts about him initially did not go much further than that. He seemed pleasant and had a good sense of humour based on the short banter, and I determined, from what my friend had shared, that he was a 'cool' guy who always gave a helping hand when he could. For him, however, our exchange would not end there, as I found out long after that he had returned to my friend's house later that day to inquire about me.

When our mutual friend invited us both over to her house for soup on a Saturday evening, I felt myself being open with slight apprehension— the kind that has no real basis except having a negative view of what appeared to be an attempt at "match-making." I think in the back of our minds, people consider this as somewhat beneath them because it can feel like a 'desperate' measure. However, being "set up" has its merit. Many couples form a lasting connection because of a simple introduction or referral. Once there are healthy boundaries and respect between both parties, then the possibilities are endless.

Our first meeting involved a good mix of laughter, stirred interests, stimulating conversation, and enough commonalities to spark a small flame. He was a teacher at a prominent all-male high school in Kingston, and I was intrigued by his apparent authentic investment in his students' lives. He referred to them by their first names when sharing a few experiences.

Consequently, it came naturally for me to share about my experiences of mentoring and supporting female youth through the various initiatives I had been part of. That was followed by my sharing about my travels to China as a part of the Global Shapers Community. It did not hurt that my husband-to-be was as handsome as they come and an active runner. However, the budding spark was dampened when he shared that he was not a Christian—without my asking or anything—and when we parted that night without exchanging numbers, I was at peace that although it was an enjoyable conversation, it would probably be our last.

Fast forward a couple of weeks to when the same friend who introduced us returned and asked me if I would be okay with her giving him my number. I took a moment to think about it and reasoned with God, like, *"Lord, I really thought that last conversation was the end. I mean, why would You want me to engage a guy who, though I found attractive, outrightly stated he was not a Christian?"* In response, I somehow felt peace moving forward with exchanging numbers, and that began a whole new chapter in our lives.

As was expected, our WhatsApp conversations were engaging, and I found him quite different in many ways from other guys. For one, he did not seem to waste words. By that, I mean he would issue compliments but only ones that were meaningful and deliberate; he was direct in articulating his intentions in getting to know me, which he stated were to see what kind of spouse I could be. His forwardness took me off guard, but it was also refreshing, to be honest, especially because I realized that he was naturally this straightforward. There was no pretense nor trying to put on a front. He exercised boundaries that I had identified as areas of growth for me, like not spending endless hours on phone calls, as much as we both enjoyed our conversations. This gave me the space I needed to think, assess my feelings, observe him with right judgment; to breathe! He was really the breath of fresh air I did not know I needed. There was a contrast to the guys I had been interested in before, who were typically always pushing the envelope, wanting to see how much more they could get or how much further we could go—this guy did not try to manipulate or add any pressure during that process of us getting to know each other. I found that, if nothing else, we were developing a friendship that had a lot of potential, but there was still one prevailing issue: our differences in our relationship with God. It was the elephant in the room, but eventually, as we became more familiar with each other, it became easier to delve deeper into that aspect of our lives. I recall telling him plainly that, as a Christian, I did not believe in being married to an unbeliever, but in terms of building a friendship, I did not feel opposed. Being the person he is, with an inquiring mind and sometimes a bit controversial, he challenged my thinking at times, but more often than not, he listened and respected the values I chose to live by.

We continued to communicate via WhatsApp primarily for the next two years due to him going abroad to pursue a Master's program, and in the midst of that, God taught me patience and self-control, and He deepened my level of trust and obedience to Him. I fasted and prayed with our mutual friend every Monday for a period of time, and we were grateful to see our prayers answered as my husband-to-be made the decision to turn his life over to Christ completely (no longer partially). He was baptised when he returned to Jamaica a few months later and continued to embark on his walk with the Lord.

Later in the year, after he was baptised, he proposed on my birthday, despite the many challenges we faced that year, including the mayhem of the COVID-19 pandemic. 2020 will forever be a significant year in our lives.

I have to admit, the months leading up to being proposed to were anxiety-filled, and if I had gone with how I was feeling, I might not have even been married today. I suffered from disappointment, unmet expectations, and concerns about the relationship's longevity because there were so many problems I chose to focus on and give energy to. But God's grace and wisdom intervened, and with the help of counsellors, I was able to see what God was trying to show me all along: that He was going to take two imperfect people and form them into a unit that would honour Him and represent a counter-cultural standard of His for romantic relationships.

To this day, it feels like the Father "arranged" my union, as in the familiar Indian custom. I very often feel as though my husband and I are just getting to know each other for the first time, even though we have been in each other's lives for years. God has been taking me through a process of stripping away every romanticised idea I had about deep love shared between a man and his wife—every single one—from what I imagined my wedding and honeymoon would be, to what sex in my early years of marriage would look like and all the travel adventures my husband and I would do together. Instead, our earliest years were impacted by curfews and lockdowns for our wedding day and honeymoon; my husband was in a new job in a brand new field, earning a commission-based salary, which was stress-inducing and gave way to a host of issues around intimacy, and finally, those dreams of traveling and doing adventures together would clearly have to wait for the same reason mentioned before. So much for our plan to "enjoy" our marriage for the first two years before thinking of including children. I found myself constantly thinking: now is the time we should be doing this and that before children came into the picture, but more and more, it appeared as though all I had was this illusion of a timeline that was nothing more than that. But there are two things I am mindful of, and I had to be very intentional in holding on to this truth: that God does not withhold any good thing from us, and therefore if my romanticised ideas did not manifest in a way I imagined, it is because God has something more suitable in store than what I had pictured. It might not be all I wanted, but it will certainly be all I needed.

What rekindles my desire for my husband repeatedly is when I get to see him, like really see him with all his intelligence, his sense of humour, his simplistic ways of entertaining and being entertained, and the curiosity he piques in me due to those nuances that make us differ from each other. The truth is, the early years of marriage have been riddled with moments that make it hard for me to really see him, especially when I could only see through the lens of feeling dejected, unseen, and misunderstood. In those times, if I did not have divinely placed people in my life who could gently guide me to my Saviour while extending the utmost understanding so as not to make me feel dismissed, I do not know how I would have managed.

There is a memory I have of seeing him for the first time in over a year when he had left for school in China. We planned to meet up in Thailand, which was a good meeting point since I had been attending a conference there. The weird thing I remember was seeing him sitting in the lobby of my hotel, waiting for me to come from my room. I saw him before he saw me, I believe, and my immediate reaction internally was a queasy, uncertainty and, for all of one second, I was really not sure if I even found him attractive.

I believe feeling doubt when you are entering a new relationship is completely natural, and though sometimes the doubt is legitimate and worth exploring, it can also be fleeting and meaningless. That experience reminded me of the matchmaking hit series on Netflix, Love is Blind, where couples get engaged after a few days of getting to know each other behind a screen or "in the pods," as the show calls it. After meeting in person for the first time and spending more real-time together, they would confess all kinds of conflicting feelings during that first-sight process. In my case, I had been familiar with how he looked, of course, but it had been over a year after all. Despite the queasy feeling, I gradually felt better about my choice as I walked towards him and was confident that happiness awaited. He greeted me with a sweet Chinese gift, and we spent the rest of the night exploring some of Bangkok's nightlife in the company of the group of friends I was there with. He stayed in a hotel not far from where I was staying, so the next day, when I was checking out of the hotel where we were accommodated for the duration of the conference, he excitedly met me bright and early in the lobby as we anticipated the next 2-3 days of adventure. It would be three of the most amazing days of our lives that could never be recaptured. At that moment, life was truly bliss. He had a chance to take a break from his studies, and I had the next couple of days to focus on being a tourist—away from work and conference stuff.

The first order of business was to get me situated in another hotel, which was managed by one of my Thai colleagues whom I met on the trip. We grabbed a taxi, accompanied by my new Colombian bestie, whom I met only days before. After having lunch together, she bid us adieu, and now it was just us left to do whatever we wanted. We found my hotel, dropped off my bags, and examined my room, which was chic, minimalistic, and just right—not surprising when you are in the hub of hospitality in my books. South East Asia, particularly Thailand, exposed me to a dimension of warmth and customer service that I have yet to find elsewhere. It holds a special place in my heart because of this. And yet, could it

144

have simply been a special grace from God extended to both of us, as He knew this trip would eventually play a significant role in the destiny of our future together? Who knows. All I can say is that the experience was magical, and it remains one of our fondest memories of travel.

After we rested my bags, we wasted no time seeing more of Bangkok, so we went to the streets. We took in the sights of restaurants on every corner, street vendors selling different foods on sticks, busy roadways, and people walking. We popped into a 7-Eleven that we spotted and bought some travel essentials, including bottles of water. We took pictures, and in no time, the hours passed; the next thing I remember was stopping by a pizza joint, basically across from my hotel, where we ate dinner and tried to map out how we wanted to spend the remainder of the trip. I had always envisioned elephants being part of the plan in some way, although I was conscious about visiting a sanctuary where the elephants were taken care of and not exploited. We spoke to a representative at my hotel who pointed us to the perfect arrangement: a full-day package that came complete with a driver for the day who would be driving us a few hours outside of Bangkok, entry to the elephant haven, and lunch at the location.

We set out at about 6:00 am. Demar met me in the lobby, and we waited as our driver approached in a modern, black Prado—definitely a more luxurious car than I had imagined. Our driver was down-to-earth and pleasant. He offered to make stops on the way, and he gladly waited as we toured a market and had a chance to take in more of the local landscape in a more rural region. Our driver offered to stop at the Kanchanaburi War Cemetery, which happened to be on the way. It is a beautiful historical site dedicated to the victims of Japanese imprisonment while building the Burma Railway. Even if we had not fully appreciated the history of such a place then, since we had just learned about it, it still felt special to have been there and to take pictures. But this would be just the beginning of our typical tourist photo-taking on that day. We could not believe how much we had done, courtesy of our driver/tour guide, who managed to get us to the elephant haven in time for the start of the activities there, despite how many stops we made. Our hearts were full.

The day of activities with the elephants began with us first standing in an open-air, grassy space with other patrons, surrounded by a group of elephants of all sizes who were being fed tall stalks of grass. We were told that this sanctuary focused on serving elephants who had been 'discarded' by previous owners and were no longer being cared for, roaming aimlessly, and some who were very elderly and unable to care for themselves anymore. It was amazing to witness the majesty of these creatures and yet to see them in a natural habitat, living so free…so happy. It made me happy to be participating in a process that protected such sacred animals that I had never interacted with in person this closely.

Next, we were led to an area for selecting fruits to be washed for the baby elephants. These included small watermelons and a vegetable called Yam Bean, which we had not seen before. It is a root vegetable with brown skin but white on the inside that tastes almost like an apple but slightly less sweet. Apparently originating from Mexico, it is also known as Mexican Turnip. We set aside the fruits in good condition, separate from those that were bruised, and when we were finished sorting, we went off to another set of activities. The day was filled with enough things that allowed us time with the elephants and time connecting as a group.

Demar connected with a Taiwanese man and his girlfriend, and he spoke in Mandarin about his studies in China. Our new friends were impressed, and soon, it seemed like the two men were bound to be friends for life. There is something about travel and the unique way it draws travellers into a bond much faster and more meaningfully than when meeting in an ordinary way. Something about beholding the wonder of a country and its culture together, while experiencing the bewilderment and typical fears that are associated with being in an unfamiliar place that makes us more vulnerable and reliant on each other.

The highlight of the day had to be when the time came to change into swimwear to join the elephants in a lake, which, under normal circumstances, I probably would not have stepped foot in, let alone my entire body. But swimming with the elephants and the rest of the group of fellow tourists was a unique experience I would never trade for the world. The inexplicable joy it brought us and the happiness that seemed to exude from the over-excited animals who drew in water with their trunks and sprayed, or some simply stood calmly while the curious two-legged creatures used brooms to gently scrub their backs and pour buckets of water on them. The time was blissful and surreal, bringing me peace that would make it one of my most treasured memories.

Our driver waited for us at the location the entire day and took us back to my hotel—all part of the service covered in the one-time fee we paid. Needless to say, I would highly recommend the experience to anyone visiting Bangkok or any other part of Thailand. Our roughly three-hour non-stop ride home was the perfect way to unwind after a full day of activities, and when the driver offered his stereo to play our choice of music, I grasped the opportunity to play some Christian worship tunes; after such a glorious day, my heart could burst with gratitude to God.

As if the day had not been wonderful enough, we got home in time to tick one more thing off our Bangkok Bucket List. The city is well-known for its breathtaking sky bars, and we wanted a taste of the nightlife before our time in Thailand came to an end. We did a Google search and found a popular spot that wasn't too far from us—after all, we were understandably still tired, and neither of us was looking for any more adventure, which taking public transportation in a foreign country that speaks another language can sometimes be. So, we opted to keep it as simple as possible.

We entered Banyan Tree, and the first order of business was to grab some pictures with the venue's beautiful aesthetic;

then we went to change some cash at the front desk, and by the time we made it to the seating area where we had to wait for a good seat, we were told that the main kitchen was closing and that the time for serving alcohol was about to end. The country would have been celebrating a Muslim holiday the following day, and therefore, at the stroke of midnight, alcohol serving would cease. That was a culture shock if I had ever seen one. We managed to order some drinks before the cut-off time, but we missed the kitchen, which meant having to grab some bite-sized items, which left me feeling underwhelmed. If I had felt adventurous, I would have suggested that we grab some street food, but knowing my limits with travel and hesitation with food from a roadside, I opted for the safer route. Nevertheless, the main attraction was, after all, the view we had from the sky bar; our seat was perfectly nestled in a corner with large windows that gave us the perfect panorama of the city as we hugged and took it all in.

The next day would have been our final day in Thailand and the last time we would be spending together before not seeing each other again for months. Demar still had roughly half a year of his studies to go, and none of us really wanted to face that reality at that moment. We spent the day relaxing mostly at my hotel, where we ate, swam in the pool, and even worked out for a bit at the hotel's small gym. My flight was scheduled for very early the following morning, and I had to leave my hotel at about 10:00 pm that night, so we spent the afternoon at a mall where we got a few souvenir items. I got a mixture of unusual Asian-inspired tropical clothing, some costume jewelry, intricately shaped soaps, and a few fridge magnets—just whatever my remaining budget could salvage. I have never been one to focus on souvenirs when I travel. I am all about racking up the experiences, splurging on that if need be, and making sure to capture the memories, whether with pictures or videos—those are the souvenirs for me. But travelling so far from home compels you to bring back at least something tangible as a reminder of the time spent, and you feel compelled to bring something back, whether big or small, for family members and close friends. Going to the mall was the perfect way to conclude the trip because in the food court was a section dedicated to Thai "street food"—a dream come true, I thought, since I had been so sceptical of eating the food from the actual street. I did yearn to try some of the foods I had heard about. My culinary experience in Thailand had been top-tier quality, considering the foods we ate during the time of the conference, and I did not want anything to ruin my impression, so when the opportunity came, I sampled some street food delicacies, including servings of crispy pork, fish balls, pork ribs, pimento chicken and papaya salad, which is a Thai essential.

Before we knew it, it was time to head back to the hotel to pack my bags and get ready to head to the airport, alone—a journey I dreaded more and more by the second. We gathered my things; the next thing I knew, it was time to leave.

Our driver from the elephant excursion was designated to transport me to the airport which was a distance away—

another reason I had to leave relatively soon after arriving back at the hotel. I said my goodbyes to my love, fighting back the tears. We embraced and stopped counting the minutes. Then I sat in the back seat of the Pajero, the same seats we shared a day ago, having the most memorable time of our lives together. As the car turned out of the driveway and we began the journey to the airport, a sadness engulfed me that I will never be able to put into words. I sobbed for what felt like hours, not caring about how concerned my driver, who knew very little English, might have felt. I pretty much cried myself into a stupor. I woke up when my driver pulled into the departure section of the airport. He had been so accommodating, so gentle in light of my crisis. Despite the language barrier, he knew why I was sad, and he empathised. He helped me with my things, and I managed to thank him for all he had done while wishing him all the best.

The next few hours were spent trying hard to contain myself enough to correspond with the flight staff and make sure that I was all set for my route back home, which would entail a layover in Tokyo for about eight hours, then to New York, and finally Kingston, Jamaica. In between my wait time, I logged on to the airport WiFi and made a few calls to Demar. It comforted me to hear his voice, and he expressed his own sadness at us having to say goodbye after such a wonderful time, even if it would just be for a few months. He was actually slated to stay one more day in Bangkok, and then he would be on his way back to Beijing. As I recall this story, it all sounds dramatic, even to me, with all the crying and overwhelming sadness, but it truly was a kind of heaviness that

I had not experienced before in relation to "a guy" who was outside of a breakup. So, I was taken off guard by my own reaction to the situation. It made me think, what could this mean? Is this just a meaningless response that should not be read into? Or am I feeling this intense level of separation anxiety because I have found "my person?" I could not help but wonder.

When I had a chance, I mentioned to a handful of close friends that I was officially off the market. I shared that Demar asked me to be his girlfriend while on the trip, and I told him yes. My friends were generally ecstatic at the news. One friend shared that she went to bed asking God for a positive dream (after having a series of unpleasant ones prior to that), and she did have a good dream of Demar and I coming together as a couple. This happened without her knowing how my time was going with Demar while on the trip. Another friend who was more concerned than anything else initially expressed, *"But why did you say yes if you do not know what the status of his relationship with God is?"* knowing how important it was to me to be on the same page in that regard. I explained that, firstly, I had conversations with him on our trip about his faith, and based on what he shared about his church involvement and small Bible Study group participation at his school, I was confident that he was showing interest and actively taking steps in the right direction. Additionally, I prayerfully approached this decision and felt a sense of peace about proceeding with being his girlfriend, at least. After all, while being a girlfriend is a commitment, it is not a lifelong vow, and I maintained that if we seemed to be going in different directions, we both were free to end the relationship. Unlike in marriage, when things are not as simple as that. I had hoped that would have been the end of having to explain my decisions to some of the people closest to me who had my best interest at heart, but it was only the beginning. That period taught me there is a cost to listening keenly to God's voice and following His direction, and not everyone will understand or agree with your choices. What is most important is to ensure His voice is resounding loudest in your ear.

SPOKEN FOR BY GOD

My God!
You cause me to laugh uncontrollably;
my strength is truly the joy of the Lord!
There is nothing I face that makes me worry,
nor can any man thwart my peace,
for You are the Giver of life.
The heavens and the earth declare that You are Lord.

The trees outstretch their limbs to praise You,
the birds soar without knowing how they will be fed,
the seas billow at Your beck and call—
they are made to stop wherever You instruct.
The storms are powerless at the raising of Your hand,
and the sun gives light upon Your words: "Let there be light."

You provide such protection;
not even I can cause my own harm,
for like a blanket, You cover me,
shielding me from the perils of my own shortcomings.
My insecurities fall prey to Your all-encompassing love.
What an awesome God You are!

You are love personified.
I have known the look, smell, and taste of it.
Love is beyond the sweet and alluring aroma of my coffee,

beyond the taste of satisfaction as my thirst is forever
quenched.
Love is the sight of You, Jesus;
it is the freedom of being Your child.

Love is in the skies—
the light, pillow-formed soft clouds on a bright day,
the mighty and powerful bursts of thunder,
pregnant with Your magnificence.
It is the vibrance in the life around us,
the humming of everyday hustle and bustle.

It is in the light,
where darkness cannot thrive—
uncontainable, reckless, unbiased as it shines.
Even in the depths of hell, Your light shines;
evil shudders at the mention of the name—
Jesus, King, Messiah, Lord of lords, King of kings.

My God! My God! How great You are.
Though the snare of the devil is upon us,
and daily, he seeks to devour and destroy,
still Your victory over the earth
remains undefiled, unrivaled, victorious.
God of redemption! You saved my soul.

When the distorted words penetrate our skulls,
infest our minds, and contaminate our temples,
Your Word, like a sharp-edged knife, is able to pierce us.
It repairs and comforts, reproves yet restores.

It seeks out the lost, even without their looking.
Your Word is a light to my feet, music to my ears,
a sword in my hand—yet sweeter than honey.

PERSONAL REFLECTION

Have you ever felt so overwhelmed with gratitude to God for what He has done in your life? Proclaim it in the form of a poem or any other written form here:

_____

_____

_____

_____

_____

_____

_____

_____

_____

_____

_____

_____

_____

_____

_____

_____

Epilogue

Is it possible to break cycles or patterns of behaviour in our romantic pursuits that invariably lead to heartbreak? Absolutely, yes. Does this mean we can avoid all instances of heartbreak, even when there are factors we cannot control? The answer is no. Immunity to heartbreak is not possible if you are a living, healthy human being with feelings. However, the role we have to play in the heartbreak, as well as how well we recover from it, are the things we can tackle.

The reality is that even my husband—the man I believe the Lord led me to marry; the man with whom I have shared a relationship that has been devoted to God, albeit imperfectly—has caused me heartbreak. Whether knowingly or unknowingly, intentional or not, my husband has caused me deep emotional pain, and that is because he is flawed, and so am I. It can feel stifling knowing that I cannot resort to old patterns or habits of coping with that kind of pain because those ways are maladaptive in marriage. In singleness, I could opt out if I wanted to at any point, but in Christian marriage, we are called to a counter-cultural approach to handling this life-long commitment.

The lessons I have shared in this book that I applied during the better part of my single years, I am being challenged to continue to apply in marriage. That is the gospel truth: that we never stop needing the love of our heavenly Father, and no one can ever—nor should ever—take the place of our loving Saviour, Jesus.

When I talk about marriage these days, I find myself talking about Jesus more than I talk about my spouse. Not intentionally so, but it is almost like he is on the periphery of this adventure (marriage) that I am experiencing with the Lover of my soul. I go to Him to complain, just as I go to Him to giggle about things my husband does and says that are sweet or utterly ridiculous. I know this may all sound weird, and maybe some people reading may feel deflated at the fact that this is what the reward is at the end of the day. On the other end of your praying and believing God for marriage is *the reward of more of Jesus.*

I think of Hannah, whose womb was closed up by God, the Bible says, but Hannah pleaded with God out of her desperation, and she vowed if God gave her a child, she would dedicate that child to the service of the Lord for all the days of his life (see 1 Samuel). When she gave birth to her son, she did not forget the Lord or her vow to Him. Instead, she insisted that she must honour her word as a function of her faithfulness to the Lord. Her reward at the end of her praying was not just the gift of a son, but the gift of a son who she could faithfully return unto the Lord as she vowed because she knew that would please Him—which was her priority above all.

How different would our marriages be if we went into them with that kind of outlook and focus, as Christians, that the aim for pursuing marriage is to have even more intimacy with Jesus above everything else; above living your best life on exotic trips with bae, having the most romantic dates, the best sex of your life, building an empire together, even expanding your family. It is critical that we adjust our outlook and motives for marriage to focus on Jesus, not because the desires previously mentioned are bad but because they are fickle and easily influenced by a myriad of variables that we do not control.

The couple that cannot go on trips together due to an unexpected event like a global pandemic or maybe an accident that rendered you or your spouse disabled; the couple that lacks ingenuity after the early days of sweetness wear off, who cannot seem to come up with romantic things to do made worse by financial challenges; the couple that is poorly managing the stresses of life which impacts their sexual relationship; the couple of two fiercely independent individuals who are busy building their own brands and cannot seem to come together to establish a joint entity; the couple who has issues with infertility or other complications that impede their ability to have children—these among other scenarios describe the painful circumstances facing many marriages. Is there hope for these marriages? Can they survive the insufferable disappointment and disillusionment that would have set in based on the expectations they had going into marriage? Can the marriage still be happy without the couple compromising their Christian values?

Believe me, I present this not with the intention of pouring cold water on your aspirations for happiness. I am a visionary myself, and I am energised by dreaming about wonderful things for my future also. Therefore, I empathise with feeling the tension of being an imaginative person and, at the same time, having to maintain a sober perspective on the realities of marriage, not to mention how much my limited amount of experience being married has forced me to face the music. The past couple of years have shown me the futility of these things we strive for and how much we allow our joy to be robbed when they are not fulfilled in the way we imagine. The most salient lesson I have been learning is this: *"My hope (my dreams, expectations, etc.) is built on **nothing** less than **Jesus' blood and righteousness,** and I dare not trust the sweetest frame (the things my limited mind has perceived) but wholly trust in Jesus name."*

I may not have realised it then, but when I began that journey of praying for my husband and eventually entering this union, I thought the fulfilment of that was a conclusion in a sense, but I now see that it was actually more of a beginning of sorts. It is the start of a new dimension that the Lord is taking me in my relationship with Him—a dimension of even more stripping away of the things in me that are not of Him, a place of more healing of the deeply inflicted wounds, a place of my eyes being further opened where I am able to receive the wisdom I have prayed for. If I could just see marriage as a continuation of the best adventure of my life, that is, my walk with the Lord Jesus; the One I have travelled solo with all over the world, the One who has gifted me with talents that have ushered me into all kinds of spaces and platforms, the One who connected me with people and gave me relationships that changed my life in a multitude of ways, and the One who promised and gave me a husband to fulfil His purposes. He is the One who has never left me. From my childhood, when emotional abandonment and rejection threatened, He called me His. As I am writing this, tears of gratitude flow as I consider how much the Saviour loves me. What can this world take from me when I have Jesus?

This is the perspective I desire for you to have, my single sister in Christ, and you must keep this at the forefront of your mind, even more so as you prepare your mind and heart for marriage. The fulfilment of God's promises is an ongoing work that never stops. Even when you have the reward of what you have prayed for, know that there is more that the Lord has for you to receive, and that reward is just the beginning.

"Indescribable Feeling" is the first poem I wrote in relation to heartbreak during my years in high school.

Indescribable Feeling

It's a feeling I can't describe.
A feeling of sweet doubt and anxiety,
as I anticipate what happens next.
The days pass by slowly when we are together,
giving me enough time to decide my destiny...
I treasure these memories.

It's a feeling I can't describe.
The way my body moves when I'm around you—
I feel like a child exploring new things,
so curious to know where my feelings will take me.
Predicting the outcome will be one that I'll regret,
and yet, I treasure these memories.

It's a feeling I can't describe.
One minute I'm happy,
the next I'm sad,
no longer in control of my own emotions,
but now a victim of so-called "love."
Still, I treasure these memories.

164

It's a feeling I can't describe.
The way I loathe the mere thought of all we shared,
but in my heart, I wish we could recapture those times.
The way I sneer when you happen to pass me,
and yet, when you're not around, I long to see you.
It's amazing how one person can be the cause of your happiness,
and within the same second, be the cause of your sadness.
And how I treasure these memories.

It's a feeling I can't describe.
We get so caught up with infatuation,
ignoring all the signs that blatantly present themselves,
paying no attention to each other's flaws,
creating our own little world of perfection.
Until reality hits us—
we realize our fantasy land of "love"
now stands as a figment of our imagination,
a lie that has evolved into a memory worth being treasured.

This poem is dedicated to a beautiful multiple survivor of child sexual abuse and rape who is one of the main inspirations behind my work with Girls First International. This is a poem for sexual assault survivors.

Shelly

Look up, Shelly!
Don't you see?
Yes, you have seen hell's fury,
but you have the victory!

Long before birth, evil had its eye on you,
and from the age of five,
your innocence was robbed—and your self-worth too.
Continuous indiscretions from the ones you loved
caused you to believe deeply that it would never stop.

But look up, Shelly!
There is a fighter in you.
While you refused to remain silent,
your power began to strengthen.
And even if you only told one person,
it would be the start of your phoenix rising.

Your healing has been on its way.

We can question why it has taken so long,
but it would be wasted energy.
Pages burned with your words,
retaliating against your experience,
are the evidence of your resilience—
rejecting the lie that this was your destiny.

Look up, strong girl,
for your pain is not wasted.
As you walk away from all of this unscathed,
like the Hebrew boys, unburnt in the fire,
your life is a testimony,
a beacon of light for all to see—
that Greater is He that is in you and me!

My dear friend,
as you keep looking up,
those looking on will look up too.

About the Author

Stephanie Hazle Lyle has always been passionate about seeing women chart the path to wholeness. As a Christian creative and founder of the non-profit organization, Girls First International, she has led various initiatives that focus on the physical, emotional, mental, and spiritual well-being of girls and women, especially those who have faced trauma.

In her book *Spoken For: Unearthing God's Relentless Love and Ending the Cycle of Heartbreak*, Stephanie gives an account of life lessons, poems, and prayers around the subject of heartbreak. Her aim is to reach the hearts of Christian women who have felt disqualified from receiving and giving true love; those who have endured painful experiences and are bound by frustration around the subject of a godly marriage. From personally experiencing past relationships that ended painfully to appreciating the value of true singleness and now experiencing the faithfulness of God in her role as a wife, Stephanie hopes her story will be an example of God's goodness. Her life's journey is a picture of the relentless love of God and His interest in our "love life."

Jesus desires to walk hand in hand with us as we trust Him with every decision we make concerning the pursuit of a life partner.